CW00547850

What is to be the priority of churche[...]
with ministry pressures, pastoral ne[...]
Brownell makes a compelling case th[...]
a refreshing read as the author calls f[...]
us of the importance of being God-c[...]
area of life.

Bill James, Principal, London Seminary

What an utterly timely book! At a time when western media and intellectual
pundits are critical of and hostile to Christianity, this book is a call to once again
take seriously our identity as followers of a holy Lord and seek with all of our
might to be godly and the doers of good works. And one superlative way of doing
this is through the study of Titus, with its twin themes of godliness and good
works.

Michael A.G. Haykin, Professor of Church History,
The Southern Baptist Theological Seminary

Godliness may seem an outdated and moralistic aspect of Christianity that
leads to pietistic attitudes. Basing his study on the Letter to Titus, Brownell is
convinced that godliness brings about a "revolution" in life and that this kind
of "revolution" is what the churches desperately need in our time. The best of
evangelicalism throughout history had given priority to godliness in personal and
church life. Well-grounded in Scripture and church history, Brownell shows that
we all need godliness. Let the revolution of godliness begin afresh!

Dr Leonardo De Chirico, pastor of the evangelical church Breccia di Roma
and lecturer in Historical Theology at the Istituto di Formazione Evangelica e
Documentazione, Padova (I)

GRACE PUBLICATIONS TRUST
62 Bride Street
London N7 8AZ
www.gracepublications.co.uk

First published in Great Britain by Grace Publications Trust 2024.

Cover design by Pete Barnsley (CreativeHoot.com)

ISBN Paperback: 978-1-912154-89-0
        Ebook: 978-1-912154-90-6

Printed and bound in UK by Ashford Colour Press

The Titus Revolution

by
Kenneth Brownell

Grace
Publications

This book is dedicated to my parents, Robert and Ruth Brownell, through whom I came to faith in Christ and who by precept and example taught me what it means to be godly.

The Titus Revolution

by
Kenneth Brownell

The Titus Revolution

Contents

Godly ministry

Godly leadership

Godly lifestyle

Godly citizenship

Conclusion

Preface

This book began life as a series of sermons at East London Tabernacle Baptist Church not long before I retired as its minister. It was a kind of swan song in which I highlighted things I wanted the church to remember after I was gone. The letter of Titus had played a significant role in the life of the church. Many years ago we agreed on a church mission statement that was based on Titus and went: ELT exists to see people changed by the gospel of Jesus Christ. Our aim as a church was to see people changed for good in two senses. First, we wanted to see them changed in the most fundamental sense of being changed permanently by becoming Christians. Then, secondly, we wanted to see people changed so that they increasingly did good as they lived as Christians. In a word, we wanted people to become godly. In Titus we had a guide for doing that. Titus didn't tell us everything we needed to know about godliness; for that we need the whole of the Bible. But in Titus we had a framework for nurturing godliness that is applicable in every local church.

So, I want to thank my fellow elders, the members of ELT and the staff for their encouragement and support over the years in the mission we undertook together. I have learned so much from them and will always be thankful to God for the privilege of being their minister. Thanks too is due to Helen Gray and Jim Sayers of Grace Publications for their patience and invaluable help in getting the book to the point of being published. But most of all I am thankful to God for my family – for my wife Alison and for my children Kate and Rab, my son-in-law Philip Hammersley and my four grandsons Edward, Rory, Angus and Noah. My prayer is that these boys will grow up to become godly men in the way Paul describes in his letter to Titus.

Introduction

This book is a modest attempt to help recover nurturing godliness as fundamental to what local churches should be about. Many things clamour for attention in every church. People have needs of various kinds – spiritual, practical, emotional and more. Non-Christians need to be evangelised. Money needs to be raised to support the work. Bad relationships need to be repaired. More could be mentioned, but I think you get the point if you are familiar with church life. These are issues common to Christians and churches in every time and place. Added to that, in 'the West' there are also the challenges coming from a culture that is rapidly losing what Christian bearings it had and that sees orthodox Christianity as bad. The cross-pressures on churches in areas of sexual morality are particularly acute, especially when it comes to homosexuality and transgenderism. Christians in the 'Global South' are often minorities facing various levels of persecution or living in very politically and economically challenging circumstances. There are also the issues arising from cultures shaped by other religions such as Islam, Hinduism and Buddhism. But in whatever culture Christians find themselves and churches meet, the nurturing of godliness must be central.

What is godliness? For some it has a negative connotation as an affected form of spirituality with an old-fashioned feel to it. For others the connotations of godliness are more positive but still suggest a rather tame and quiet way of being a Christian. It doesn't seem very exciting in the way that discipleship does. But I contend that far from being old-fashioned, affected, tame, quiet and unexciting, godliness as understood from the Bible is about the deep and radical change that begins to happen when a person is converted and continues through the rest of their life. My definition of godliness is *devotion to God actively expressed in a good life empowered by the gospel.* At its heart godliness is devotion to God. The godly life is one that is focused on the triune God and out of reverence and gratitude seeks to please him. And such a life can't be passive; it must be active as a Christian nurtures or cultivates all that it means to be good according to what God has revealed in the Bible, the guide to godliness.

Thought of that way, godliness is about far more than activities we might think of as religious in the narrow sense of the word. It's about more than going to church, praying, reading the Bible and living a moral life. A godly Christian will do those things that characterise the godly life, but they will also be devoting the whole of their life from their heart to God. What the Christian does, feels and thinks will be directed to glorifying God and enjoying him. That will involve not only their personal life, but also life with other Christians in the church, as well as engagement with non-Christians in the world.

Of course, no Christian will be perfectly godly in this life. Every day sin needs to be confessed and forgiveness sought on the basis of the finished work of Christ. But progress in godliness is possible. That's why it is important to understand that godliness is empowered by the gospel. The gospel is the message of what God has done in Jesus Christ to save sinners and is, as Paul writes in Romans 1:16, 'the power of God that brings salvation to everyone who believes'. That power is exercised in the process of conversion when spiritually dead people are made alive and given new birth, but it also continues to be exercised throughout the Christian life. By the indwelling Holy Spirit God empowers every believer to live a good life, to be godly. Put another way, godliness is the reality of the new covenant whereby God puts his Spirit in those who trust in Christ so that they are moved to obey his law that he has written in their hearts (Jer. 31:33; Ezek. 36:26; Rom. 8:4).

Godliness cannot be separated from grace. Sometimes talk about godliness can be much about what we do to become godly and little of what God has done for us in Christ and is doing in us by the Holy Spirit. That is wrong. It is the gospel of God's grace in Jesus Christ that empowers godliness. We must never forget that. If we do, the Christian life becomes dutiful and joyless drudgery. But when we remember and appropriate every day the grace of God in the gospel, when we preach that gospel to ourselves and receive it by faith, we are not only able but delight to do what God commands so that we live a godly life.

Godliness, then, is at the heart of what it means to be a Christian. It is what Jesus means when he speaks of taking up our cross and following him as one of his disciples (Mk. 8:34–38) and that he so memorably describes in his Sermon on the Mount (Mt. 5–7). It is the life of faith that Paul describes so richly in his letters as he unpacks the significance of the gospel for living as Christians. It's what James means by looking 'into the perfect law that gives liberty and continuing in it' (Jas. 1:25). It's what Peter describes when he writes of how God 'has given us everything we need for a godly life through our knowledge of him who called us through his glory and goodness' (2 Pet. 1:3). It is what the writer of the Letter to the Hebrews means when he exhorts us to 'continually offer to God a sacrifice of praise – the fruit of lips that praise his name' (Heb. 13:15). It is what John means in exhorting us to walk in the light and in the truth (1 Jn. 1:7; 2 Jn. 4). But it is in his pastoral letters (1 and 2 Tim. and Tit.) that Paul very explicitly employs the word 'godliness' ten times. In one particularly memorable passage Paul exhorts his younger colleague Timothy to be godly amid the challenge of confronting false teaching and fulfilling the ministry to which he had been called. Paul writes in 1 Timothy 4:7–8,

> Have nothing to do with godless myths and old wives' tales; rather, train yourself to be godly. For physical training is of some value, but godliness has value for all things, holding promise for both the present life and the life to come.

The 'godless myths and old wives' tales' refers to the false teaching that was prevalent in Ephesus and that Timothy was to deal with. Rather than be affected by false teaching Timothy was to train himself to be godly. The Greek word that is translated 'train' is the one from which our English word 'gymnasium' is derived. Paul is telling Timothy to head for the spiritual gym and have a good workout as if in training for an athletic competition of some kind. Such spiritual training requires discipline and determination.

Paul admits that physical training has advantages for the present life – something some of us would do well to take to heart! But, godliness has advantages for both the present and future life. In the present life we deepen and grow in our relationship with God as we become more like Jesus, which puts us in a good place whatever our circumstances. Contrary to what some false teachers say, then as now, godliness isn't a means to financial gain (1 Tim. 6:5), but rather it is about being content with our circumstances (1 Tim. 6:6). As for the future life, by training ourselves to be godly we lay up treasure in heaven for ourselves as a firm foundation for the coming age in the new creation so that we may take hold of the life that is truly life (1 Tim. 6:19). What Paul exhorted Timothy to do we are to do. Train yourself to be godly.

Where such training in godliness happens is in the local church. Of course, each of us has a personal responsibility in this area and must do what is necessary to grow in the grace and knowledge of the Lord Jesus as daily we pray, meditate on God's Word, seek to please God and do good in the way we live. But we also need to train with other Christians. If you like, in the church we have godliness gym buddies. In gyms or while doing physical exercise people often train together in order to encourage and help one another. So it should be in local churches. As we make use of the corporate means of grace – the reading and preaching of the Word, singing psalms, hymns and spiritual songs, praying, coming to the Lord's Table, and using our gifts to build other Christians up as we share our lives together – we train ourselves and one another in godliness. This is why church is so important. None of us has the ability to be godly on our own.

In the light of what we have been seeing, it is not surprising that at times of spiritual recovery in the history of the church, godliness has been emphasised. This was particularly the case in the time of the Protestant Reformation in the sixteenth century and Puritan era in the seventeenth century. One of the most important books to come out of the Reformation was John Calvin's *Institutes of the Christian Religion*. Contrary to what many think, the *Institutes* is not a dry compendium of theology, but rather a beautifully written and engaging work that unfolds the evangelical faith in a way that stimulates the mind and also warms the heart. It is a deeply devotional work. Calvin's purpose in writing the book was to promote godliness, as he wrote in his preface addressed to the French king Francis I: 'My purpose was solely to transmit certain rudiments [or basics] by which those who are touched with any zeal for religion might be shaped to true godliness'.[1] This godliness he defines as 'that reverence joined with love which the knowledge of his benefits induces'.[2] In other words, godliness or reverential love for God and for people is the fruit of believers increasingly knowing him and the benefits or blessings of his salvation in Jesus Christ. Later he writes: 'The whole life of Christians ought to be a sort of practice of godliness'.[3]

Godliness embraces everything in life. Commenting on Calvin and the other Reformers' understanding of godliness or what they term 'piety', Joel Beeke and Mark Jones write:

> The sixteenth century Reformers, most notably John Calvin, would be shocked to see how poorly piety [that is, godliness] is regarded today, even among those who profess to be Reformed. For Calvin, piety involves developing right attitudes to God. It flows out of theology, and includes heartfelt worship, saving faith, filial fear, prayerful submission, and reverential love.[4]

In Calvin's wake other Reformers, and later the Puritans, followed. Exemplifying the outlook of the latter the commentator Matthew Poole, appropriately commenting on Titus 1:1, says that 'the knowledge of the truth ... is productive of a godly life, lying in [or consisting of] the true worship of God, and a universal obedience to God's will'.[5] In almost all that they wrote, that is what the Puritans promoted in the life of individual Christians – in the family and personal relationships, in the church and in the world – leaving us with a rich heritage of spirituality to benefit from today. In what he writes of one of the heirs of the Puritans in the eighteenth century, Jonathan Edwards, J. I. Packer sums up this glorious tradition:

Godliness is a matter of glorifying the Creator by humble dependence and a thankful obedience. In Christian terms, acknowledging our complete dependence upon God, as for life and health, so for grace and glory, and loving and praising and serving him for all that he has so freely given us through his Son.[6]

The way I want to help recover the nurturing of godliness as a priority for the church today is by working our way through Paul's short letter to Titus. I prefer this expository approach rather than a thematic one as it grounds our thinking in the text of Scripture. The word 'godliness' (*eusebeian* in Greek) is mentioned only once in the first verse of chapter one, but the whole letter is Paul's instructions to Titus to do what was necessary to see that godliness was nurtured among the new Christians on the island of Crete. However, it was not only in local churches on Crete that godliness was nurtured but all over the Roman Empire, as slowly but increasingly people understood and took to heart the gospel of God's grace and its implications for life. As a result a revolution began that changed the world.

In his book *Destroyer of the Gods*, Larry Hurtado shows how this happened in the centuries after the New Testament period. Based on widely accepted estimates, Hurtado says that from relatively few Christians in AD 40 there were between five and six million by AD 300.[7] Around AD 200, the north African church father Tertullian wrote with maybe a bit of exaggeration: 'We are but of yesterday, and we have filled every place among you — cities, islands, fortresses, towns, market-places, the very camp, tribes, companies, palace, senate, forum, — we have left nothing to you but the temples of your gods'.[8]

What happened? Well, in keeping with the mandate and promise of the risen and exalted Lord Jesus, Christians went to the nations beginning in Jerusalem preaching the gospel and making disciples in the power of the Spirit. But Hurtado explains that as well as preaching and teaching the gospel, Christians were distinct in Roman culture. They had a faith, that is a body of beliefs and practices, which was not 'religion' as commonly understood. They had a unique identity that transcended ethnic and social differences as it focused on Jesus Christ as the incarnate Son of God to whom they owed supreme allegiance. They had a book, the Bible, that had supreme authority as the Word of God. And they had a distinctive lifestyle shaped by the gospel that made them different from others.[9] It was that distinctiveness wedded to the preaching of the gospel that turned the world upside down. But it took time and required patient and persevering trust in God to work on his timescale.[10]

What I propose in this book is that what happened on Crete and elsewhere in the early church can and should happen today. There can be what I call the Titus Revolution beginning in every local church. It may not seem very significant or that much is happening, but if in local churches we take to heart what Paul wrote to Titus we can expect God to work in power to advance his kingdom. In his sovereignty that can happen rapidly as in the early church, or in First and Second Awakenings in eighteenth and nineteenth century Europe and North America, or in Korea and China and sub-Saharan Africa in the twentieth and twenty-first centuries. At other times and in other places, as in Europe and other western countries today, the advance is relatively slow or non-existent as many of the older denominations decline. But our God is sovereign and we can trust him to work for his glory and the good of his people.

Our job is to be faithful as we prayerfully preach and teach the gospel and nurture godliness in our generation. And in Paul's letter to Titus we have a framework for doing just that. Many things that may concern some of us are not mentioned – public worship, the Lord's Supper, and spiritual gifts, to mention only three things. Perhaps the most notable absence is anything of significance on prayer. But it seems to me that from what we read about Paul in Acts and pick up in his letters we can conclude that he took prayer for granted when writing to Titus. That may not be true of many of us. All that we read of here about nurturing godliness must be wedded to passionate prayer. By prayer we activate the outworking of God's purposes as expressed in his promises in our lives and those of others and in our churches and world. Give yourself to prayer as you give yourself to nurturing godliness in your life and church so that the revolution that began on Crete continues until the Lord Jesus returns in power and glory.

Questions for discussion

1. What comes into your mind when you hear the word 'godliness'?

2. Do you think that godliness is emphasised too much or too little in contemporary evangelical churches?

3. Do you agree with the definition of godliness as 'devotion to God actively expressed in a good life empowered by the gospel' and the way that is unpacked?

4. Are you convinced that there can be a Titus Revolution today just as much as there was in the early church?

Godly ministry

Chapter 1

Godliness is the aim of gospel ministry
(Titus 1:1–4)

One of my favourite museums in London is the Victoria and
Albert in South Kensington. From time to time, I take people
on a tour of several of its galleries, to show them the impact
of Christianity on Europe and through Europe on the world.
Beginning with an item from the Roman Empire, in which Jesus
was born and the early church grew, the tour ends with one of
the great pictures by the Renaissance painter Raphael. This is
part of a series Raphael did as templates for the tapestries he
was commissioned to do for the Sistine Chapel in the Vatican,
illustrating events from the lives of the apostles Peter and
Paul. I highlight the picture of Paul preaching in the Areopagus
in Athens as recorded in Acts 17 to show that what we need
in Europe today is preaching like that of Paul in Athens, that
brought the gospel to Europe and profoundly changed both

individual lives and whole societies in ways we still live with today.

A recent book that shows how this happened is Tom Holland's *Dominion*. Holland speaks of Christianity having a strange power that

> remains as alive as it has ever been. It is manifest in the great surge of conversions that has swept Africa and Asia over the past century; in the conviction of millions upon millions that the breath of the Spirit, like a living fire, still blows upon the world; and, in Europe and North America, in the assumptions of many more millions who would never think to describe themselves as Christian. All are heirs to the same revolution: a revolution that has, at its molten heart, the image of a god dead on a cross.[1]

Whether or not it is acknowledged or welcomed, Christianity has changed the world and done so for good. And it did so because it first changed the lives of ordinary people such as Dionysius and Damaris who, with some others, came to believe that the Jesus preached by Paul that day in Athens was the one who alone could save them from the judgment of God and give them eternal life. Believing in Jesus their lives were changed for good, as have been the lives of countless others through the centuries.

Why this happens we discover in what the apostle Paul writes as he introduces his letter to Titus. Titus was one of Paul's younger colleagues who was often tasked by him with difficult jobs. In the case of this letter, Titus had been left by Paul on the island of Crete with the job of getting churches in good order in various towns. Although not recorded in Acts it seems that Paul had at some point been preaching on Crete with the result that many people had been converted. But before he unpacks what Titus needs to do and teach, Paul reminds him, and through him the Cretan Christians, of his ministry as an apostle of Jesus Christ. As Paul puts it in verse 1, he is 'a servant of God and an apostle of Jesus Christ'. Paul is literally a slave or a bondservant, a *doulos*, of God and as such he is a man under authority. His life is not his own, but it belongs to God as his Lord and master.

As God's slave, Paul's ministry is that of an apostle of Jesus Christ. Although he had hated Jesus and persecuted his people Paul had been dramatically converted when he met the risen Jesus on the road to Damascus. Jesus sent Paul with a particular ministry as his apostle to the Gentiles. As such Paul joined the other apostles as one of the unique messengers of the risen Jesus who laid the foundation of the church in the truth of the gospel. This apostleship is mentioned by Paul in other letters, but here he does so in order to back up what Titus will teach and do with his authority as an apostle.

And that's why we need to take this letter seriously. What we read here is not merely the opinions of a man, but what the risen Jesus wants us to know as his people living in this world. What we read here was not only for the Christians on Crete in the first century, but for us and for Christians in every place and in every generation. But what Paul writes in this passage tells us about more than his apostleship. For while in one sense that ministry was unique to Paul as an apostle, it was also a template or pattern for the ministry of Christians and churches in every generation. Of course, no one today is an apostle like Paul, but if we believe in the gospel he preached and share the priorities he had, then our ministry as churches and as Christians will reflect his in some measure.

So, in this chapter I want us to think about our ministry as churches in the light of Paul's ministry. Only ministry like that of Paul can change people like us for good and, through us and others, change the world for good. And how the world, lost in spiritual darkness and without hope, needs such Paul-like gospel ministry; whether it is of people specifically set aside for it, such as pastors and elders, or of ordinary Christians through the church and in the world. That was the case in the first century as it still is in the twenty-first. But just as in the first century Paul-like gospel ministry began to turn the world upside down, so too in the twenty-first century can Paul-like gospel ministry turn the world upside down. From the passage there are three things about such life- and world-changing ministry.

1. The purpose of Paul's ministry – and ours

What was the purpose that drove Paul in his ministry as an apostle? What got him up in the morning and motivated him to give himself so totally, to sacrifice himself and to suffer as he did? He tells us: it was 'to further the faith of God's elect and their knowledge of the truth that leads to godliness' (v. 1). The purpose of Paul's ministry was, in a word, godliness. He wanted people to believe in Jesus for salvation and to become godly as

27

they understood the truth of the gospel. For that to happen two things were necessary: evangelism and edification. Lost people (which is everyone by nature) had to be evangelised through the preaching of the gospel and found people (that is, those who received the gospel by faith) then had to be edified or built up by that same gospel so that they became godly. The purpose of Paul's ministry is also the purpose of every local church.

Let's dig into this a bit more. The purpose of Paul's ministry is, in part, evangelism. However, he speaks of evangelism in a way that may sound strange. The 'elect' are Christians both together, as God's elect or chosen people, and individually, as those chosen or elected by God from eternity. In his mercy God has chosen people to be saved. In Ephesians 1:3–6 Paul speaks of this electing love as he praises God:

> Praise be to the God and Father of our Lord Jesus Christ ... For he chose us in him before the creation of the world to be holy and blameless in his sight. In love he predestined us for adoption to sonship through Jesus Christ, in accordance with his pleasure and will – to the praise of his glorious grace, which he has freely given us in the one he loves.

In 2 Timothy 1:9 he says something similar:

> He has saved us and called us to a holy life – not because of anything we have done but because of his own purpose and grace. This grace was given us in Christ Jesus before the beginning of time.

The doctrine of election is a mystery. Why God chooses some for salvation and not others is hidden from us. But the truth taught in Scripture is that, while we are fully responsible for our decisions as human beings, God is sovereign in choosing or electing those he saves. And those chosen by God in eternity past for salvation come to faith in Jesus in time. Having come to faith, that faith must then be strengthened and built up. Paul understands that the purpose of his ministry as an apostle is to see that happen. Indeed, he is willing, as he writes in 2 Timothy 2:10, to 'endure everything for the sake of the elect, that they too may obtain the salvation that is in Christ Jesus, with eternal glory'.

For God's elect, salvation begins when, in response to some form of preaching of the gospel, they first believe in Jesus, and it will be completed when they appear with him in glory. In his ministry as an apostle Paul's purpose is to see that those whom God has chosen come to faith in Christ. That is evangelism. Far from discouraging it, confidence in the sovereignty of God in saving people motivates evangelism and missions. In his sovereignty God uses people like us, as he used Paul, so that his elect come to faith.

However, godliness requires not only evangelism but also edification. The faith of God's elect also needs to be built up and strengthened. How does that happen? It is through 'their knowledge of the truth that leads to godliness'. In order to be strong, faith needs to be fed with the truth of the gospel much as a child needs to be fed with good, nutritious food. Paul also sees that as the purpose of his ministry as an apostle. Those who believe in Jesus need to grow in their understanding of the gospel. Contrary to what some people think, faith is not some kind of vague sense of dependence on God. No, faith through which people are saved is trust in Jesus Christ as offered in the gospel. And this gospel has content that tells us about who Jesus is and what he has done to save us. For faith to be strengthened and built up, believers must increasingly know the truth of the gospel in all its depth and richness as it is revealed in Scripture. A healthy Christian is always learning more about the gospel. The gospel is not only for the beginning of the Christian life at conversion, but for all of the Christian life. Such knowledge of the gospel is more than merely intellectual knowledge of its content, but it is also an ever deeper and experiential understanding of the gospel as it changes our lives for good. As we know the gospel in depth its life-changing power is unleashed in our lives so that we are changed for good.

That change for good is summed up in the word 'godliness'. What is godliness? My definition of godliness is: devotion to God actively expressed in a good life empowered by the gospel. It is the way the power of the gospel expresses itself in the whole of our lives as Christians. It includes 'religious' aspects of life such as prayer and public worship, but it also involves everything we think, say and do. It is the whole of our lives actively devoted to God in worship. It is what Paul means in Romans 12:1 when he exhorts us to offer up our bodies as a living sacrifice as our true and acceptable worship of God. Thought of that way godliness has, as Paul writes in 1 Timothy 4:8, promise not only for this life, but even more for the life to come. Therefore, in this life we must train ourselves to be godly much as we might train ourselves in a gym to compete in a sport of some kind. Godliness is really what the Christian life is about. Godliness is not something a few super-spiritual people are to devote themselves to, but something every Christian is to devote themselves to. Every Christian is to actively dedicate themselves to God as they live a good life empowered by the gospel. And it is the gospel that we increasingly know, as God's elect, that makes godliness possible as it strengthens us through faith in Jesus.

It was, then, the purpose of Paul's ministry as an apostle to see this happen and that must also be the purpose of the ministry in local churches. A church doesn't really have any other purpose for being a church. Building on the foundation that Paul and other apostles laid in the gospel, your church and every church is to do all it can 'to further the faith of God's elect and their knowledge of the truth that leads to godliness'. That purpose is fulfilled first in us, who are Christians and belong to the church. In all we do, individually and together as God's elect, our purpose is to become godly as our faith is strengthened and as we know the truth of the gospel. If you're a Christian that's your purpose every day of your life. And that's our purpose in everything churches do whether it is public worship, or pastoral care, or small groups or anything else.

But the purpose of a church is also to see that God's elect who do not yet believe in Jesus come to faith in him so that their faith may begin to be strengthened and they begin to know the truth that leads to them becoming godly. That is basically what evangelism, discipleship and missions are all about. The purpose of every church is not only that believers become godly, but also that unbelievers will come to faith so that they too may become godly. In a word, the purpose of a church, as it is for each of us as Christians, is 'godliness'.

2. The message of Paul's ministry – and ours

If the purpose of the ministry of a church is godliness that results from knowing the truth of the gospel as believers, what is the message of this gospel? The message of the gospel is the good news of what God has done in Jesus Christ to save sinners. In the New Testament that message is described in different ways. Here in verse 2, it is described as 'the hope of eternal life, which God, who does not lie, promised before the beginning of time'. The gospel is a message of hope.

What good news that is for a hopeless world! Living in the shadow of death people have no hope humanly speaking. The things people place their hopes in – relationships, money, politics or whatever – in the end fail them. Temporal life in this world is brief and uncertain and ends when we physically die (Ps. 39:4–7). For those who do not believe in Jesus for salvation there is only the prospect of eternal death beyond this life. That is God's judgment on us because of sin. But the gospel offers hope by telling us that for those who believe in Jesus for salvation there is the hope of eternal life – not merely life that goes on forever, but life in all its fullness in the new creation. It is the best of life in this world and more intensified and enjoyed but infinitely better and without any taint of sin. This is the hope of every Christian. Such hope is not simply a wish as the word hope is commonly understood, but rather, as always in the Bible, the confident expectation that God will do as he has promised.

And God will do as he has promised, because he is, as Paul writes, a God 'who does not lie'. Literally, God is 'the unlying God'. The nature of God is truth and therefore it is impossible for God to lie or to contradict himself. The promise of eternal life in which we hope is founded on the character of God. There cannot be a surer foundation than that. The name and honour of God are at stake in the salvation of those who trust in him. And this hope of eternal life is not only secure because of who God is, but because 'it was promised before the beginning of time'. In eternity God planned to save a people for himself and to give them eternal life.

At the heart of this plan is the eternal Son of the Father. And what God planned in eternity he has accomplished in time by sending his Son to be born, to live, to die and to rise again for the salvation of his people. By his death on the cross Jesus redeemed sinners so that when they trust in him, they will have their sins forgiven and receive eternal life. This is what God, who does not lie, promised from before the beginning of time. This is the hope promised to us in the gospel.

Is this your hope? Have you heard the message of hope in the gospel, and do you believe in Jesus Christ who is offered to you in it? If you have believed in Jesus, then you can live with hope in this hopeless world. Whatever your circumstances you have a hope unlike anything this world puts their hope in. You can live knowing that beyond this life there is eternal life in the new creation. You can live knowing that the best is yet to come. Because you have such a hope, promised before time began by the God who does not lie, you can bear with all the adversities and discouragements and heartaches that come in life. Christians are not exempt from such things. But because we have the hope of eternal life we know as Paul puts it in Romans 8:18 'that our present sufferings are not worth comparing with the glory that will be revealed in us'.

If that is your hope your life will be transformed in such a way that unbelievers will ask you 'to give the reason for the hope that you have' (1 Pet. 3:15). And it is this message of hope in the gospel that we must do all we can, individually and as a church, to make known to as many people as possible. As Christians we have the one message that our hopeless world needs to hear.

But how will that happen?

3. The focus of Paul's ministry – and ours

How are we to get this message of hope to the people who need to hear it? Through preaching. Preaching was the focus of the ministry of the apostle Paul and it must be the focus of our ministry as a church as well. Listen to how Paul describes his preaching in verse 3. The promise of eternal life has 'now at the appointed season' been 'brought to light through the preaching entrusted to me by the command of God our Saviour'. At the right time in his plan God commanded the apostle Paul to preach the gospel of his promise of eternal life to as many people as he could. He did so as 'God our Saviour' because of his purpose to save sinners through the gospel. And in doing so he had his 'appointed season'. The mystery of the gospel, that had before then been hidden, was now revealed so that not only Jewish people but people from all nations would believe in Jesus and be saved. Like the messenger bringing the good news of victory to a city from the battlefield, so Paul was entrusted by God to preach the good news of Christ's victory in saving sinners. He was to herald this good news for everyone to hear. And from what we read in the Book of Acts and in his letters that is what Paul did faithfully until his dying day (Acts 20:20).

And what Paul did in the first century we must do in the twenty-first century. It is through the preaching of the gospel that God's promise of eternal life through faith in Jesus Christ is made known. Such preaching is the focus of ministry of the whole church. Of course, the church does many other things as well as preaching the gospel. There's prayer, singing, caring for one another, doing good to people in need and more. But the focus of our ministry as churches must be preaching of the gospel.

Some in the church are specifically recognised and set aside for a ministry of preaching. In various ways that is the ministry of elders in the church as Paul mentions this in verse 9 when he writes of how they are to 'encourage others with sound doctrine and refute those who oppose it'. One or more of the elders usually has that ministry as a full-time or part-time occupation. Such vocational preaching ministries must be valued and supported not only financially but with prayer and encouragement. At the heart of church life must be a faithful and Spirit-anointed preaching ministry. But all the elders in a church preach the Word. Some do that occasionally in public, but all of them do that through pastoral conversation or Bible study or evangelism.

However, it is not only the elders, but all the members of the church who have a ministry of preaching the gospel both to other believers and to unbelievers. Preaching is not only proclaiming the Word to a congregation or in formal pastoral care, but also encouraging and admonishing one another as we speak the truth of the gospel to one another in love (Rom. 15:14; Eph. 4:15). Some members are gifted for specific preaching and teaching ministries to children and young people or older people or men or women at various stages of life. Then as we live and work in the world, we use the opportunities the Lord gives us to preach the gospel to unbelievers through conversation and in other ways. Like the early Christians we are to preach the Word wherever we go (Acts 8:4). Some Christians are gifted evangelists, but most of us simply need to use the opportunities that God gives us to speak about Jesus as we give the reason for the hope we have. In the places we live and work and play the focus of our ministry as Christians, whatever else we do, must be the proclamation of the gospel.

The amazing reality is that when we preach the gospel God is bringing to light the hope of eternal life he has promised. Through our preaching God brings hope to people. That may not be appreciated by everyone, and they may even be hostile to us if they are not Christians. But if by God's grace they believe in Jesus they will realise that through what we preached to them God has brought to light in their lives the hope of the gospel.

That's what we want to see happening more and more in our communities, in our nation and in the world. How people need the gospel in which God promises hope to those who believe in Jesus. Unlike so many of the promises made in this world, what God promises he will do. He is the God who does not lie. God never makes a promise he does not keep. To be unfaithful is contrary to his character as the God of truth. Therefore, we can trust God and know that he will keep his promise of eternal life in the gospel.

What confidence that gives us as Christians as we live in this world and what a message that gives us as we go into the world with the gospel! In our preaching we offer people the hope that the God who does not lie promised before the beginning of time to all who believe in Jesus Christ. Then when people believe they begin to know the truth that leads to godliness. That is how people are changed for good and, through them, how the world can be changed for good.

Questions for discussion

1. Are you convinced that nurturing godliness is the purpose of the ministry of every local church and its leaders?

2. How do evangelism and edification nurture godliness?

3. Why does what Paul says about the message of the gospel encourage us and give us confidence in ministry?

4. Why is preaching so important and what place must it have in church?

5. How should what Paul says about the object, message and focus of his ministry and ours shape the way we do church – in public worship, evangelism, children's and youth work, pastoral care and counselling to name five areas?

Godly leadership

Chapter 2

Godliness is established through local churches led by elders who teach the gospel (Titus 1:5–9)

Like an invading army, godliness must gain a beachhead in enemy territory. How does that happen? As we saw in the last chapter godliness was the big thing that the apostle Paul aimed for in his ministry. As he writes in verse 1, the purpose of his ministry was 'the faith of God's elect and their knowledge of the truth that leads to godliness'. Although no one since the time of Paul and the other apostles is an apostle in the sense that they were, nevertheless, the purpose of Paul's ministry remains the purpose of the ministry of churches and Christians who are faithful to the apostolic gospel. And the message of that apostolic gospel is the hope of eternal life promised before the beginning of time by God who cannot lie. Therefore, like the apostle Paul in his generation, we must in our generation have the same focus on the preaching of the gospel – the preaching by which God our Saviour brings to light the hope of the gospel.

But is such preaching of the gospel enough to establish godliness in the world? Is it enough that 'the truth that leads to godliness' is preached and that by God's grace people believe in Jesus and are saved? Important as it is, preaching the gospel is not enough. Of course, in exceptional circumstances believers in Jesus living in isolation can become godly with only a Bible and maybe not even that. But normally in God's purposes more is needed for believers in Jesus to become godly. Churches are needed and not only churches, but also leaders of those churches, where there is faithful preaching and teaching of the gospel of the apostles.

Churches and their leaders really matter. Therefore, having greeted Titus in verses 1–4, Paul launches straight into the business of establishing godliness on the island of Crete. He begins with the appointment of leaders (elders or overseers), in the churches of the various towns on the island. At some point Paul had spent time on Crete preaching the gospel. This probably happened after his imprisonment in Rome, recorded at the end of the Book of Acts. When he and perhaps others moved on, Paul left Titus behind with directions to get the new churches into order by appointing leaders who would teach the truth of the gospel. That that was Paul's priority is significant. It tells us how important it is for the establishment of godliness that there are well-led churches that teach the gospel.

And what is the godliness that is so important? As we have seen, *godliness is devotion to God actively expressed in a good life empowered by the gospel.* The establishment of godliness defined that way is the purpose of the ministry of every local church and of every Christian. We want to see such godliness being nurtured and flourishing in our churches and also spreading into the world as unbelievers come to faith in Jesus through the preaching of the gospel. That must be the purpose not only of our churches but also of every Christian. Each of us must aim to become godly – that is, to be actively expressing our devotion to God in good lives empowered by the gospel. That happens not only individually as every Christian applies the gospel to their lives, but also collectively as the gospel is preached by godly leaders in local churches.

There is a lot of confusion today about the church and its leadership and even about the gospel itself. Some people think about the church largely in terms of a building or a denominational organisation such as the Church of England or the Roman Catholic Church. Others hardly think about church at all and its place in the Christian life. Their approach to being a Christian is very individualistic and church is largely about fitting in with what works for them. It's a kind of cafeteria form of Christianity – even of the high-end kind you get in posh hotels – where you pick and choose what you want to eat. It may all seem very nice, but it can also be very unhealthy. In the church this is a form of worldliness, and in such a context commitment and accountability as a church member has little importance or meaning.

Still others talk a lot about the church but what they say has little to do with what we read in the New Testament. Leadership can be understood more in terms of models of leadership in the world rather than in terms of what is revealed in Scripture. The pastor can be seen more in terms of being a CEO or therapist or a social worker than a shepherd caring for the sheep. And as to the gospel, tragically what is taught in many churches is not the gospel revealed in the Bible but what conforms to the world's way of thinking. This is seen increasingly today as historic denominations turn away from the gospel and the life it entails as commanded in the Bible. If we are really serious about seeing godliness established in the world, then what we must do is to go back to the Bible and seek to understand what it says about the gospel and the church and her leaders.

1. To establish godliness in the world *churches* are needed

It seems that after Paul's mission on the island of Crete those who had believed in Jesus and been baptised began to meet together in the various towns on the island. Believers met together to build one another up in their new faith. Before he left, Paul had given Titus instructions to appoint leaders for these new churches. In verse 5 Paul reminds Titus of this in order to encourage him to get on with the job – 'The reason I left you in Crete was that you might put in order what was left unfinished and appoint elders in every town as I directed you'.

Before we think about these church leaders, let's focus on the churches they were to lead. The word 'church' is not mentioned but that is what Paul is concerned with. He understands that if these young believers are to become godly they need churches.

That shouldn't surprise us. After all, we know from the Book of Acts that on the Day of Pentecost the 3000 newly baptised believers were added to the church in which they 'devoted themselves to the apostles' teaching and to the fellowship, to the breaking of bread and to prayer' (Acts 2:42). It quickly became clear that church was essential for the spiritual life and witness of the new believers. As recorded in Acts, Paul and the other apostles planted churches wherever they preached, and people believed and were baptised. The letters of Paul and Peter and others in the New Testament are mostly addressed to churches facing challenges of various kinds. And central to Paul's thinking was that the church is at the heart of what God was doing in the world. As he puts it in Ephesians 3:10–11,

> [God's] intent was that now, through the church, the manifold wisdom of God should be made known to the rulers and authorities in the heavenly realms, according to his eternal purpose that he accomplished in Christ Jesus our Lord.

Church is very important in God's purposes. And in the New Testament what it means to be a church is pictured in various images. The church is pictured as a body, or as a bride, or as a temple. Here in this passage the church is pictured as a household. That's the image Paul uses in verse 7 where he writes that an elder 'manages God's household'. The image Paul has in mind is of the large household of a wealthy Roman. In Roman culture a wealthy man would appoint someone to

43

manage his home and estate with responsibility over the other servants and even over his children. Jesus uses this image in his parable of the servants waiting for their master to return from a wedding banquet. In Luke 12:42–43 Jesus says:

> Who then is the faithful and wise manager, whom the Lord puts in charge of his servants to give them their food allowance at the proper time? It will be good for that servant whom the master finds doing so when he returns.

Do you get the picture? Because the church is the household of God, we need to know how to conduct ourselves as members of it. Having written about the public worship and leadership of the church Paul tells us why these things are important in 1 Timothy 3:14–15,

> Although I hope to come to you soon, I am writing you these instructions so that, if I am delayed, you will know how people ought to conduct themselves in God's household, which is the church of the living God, the pillar and foundation of the truth.

The church is, then, one big extended family. Because the churches of the New Testament met in homes this image of the church was very real. Whatever their religious background or ethnic origin or social status in the world, believers in Jesus were members of one big extended family. They were fathers and mothers and brothers and sisters and sons and daughters to one another. As Paul told Timothy in 1 Timothy 5:1–2,

> Do not rebuke an older man harshly, but exhort him as if he were your father. Treat younger men as brothers, older women as mothers, and younger women as sisters, with absolute purity.

What was true in the early church remains true today. We are God's household as we share our lives together as Christians.

What does this mean practically when it comes to establishing godliness? It means that for godliness to be established in any place, churches that function like households are needed. Churches are not merely organisations that provide services and activities for people that they can use as they wish. Sadly, for many church can be like a self-service cafeteria where you come when you want and take what you like. That can be the case with a traditional preaching-centred church or a contemporary music-centred church. No, churches are households or families of believers who care for one another and are committed to helping one another become more godly. Key to that is the preaching of the Word in various forms and not least in the main meetings by elders, as we'll see.

But being a household or family also means praying with and for one another, doing good to one another, helping one another, encouraging one another, serving one another and much more. In this way we help one another become more godly as together we know the truth that leads to godliness. Such household-like churches are especially necessary for the establishment of godliness in hostile cultures like that of Crete. With its reputation for deceit and immorality Crete was a tough place to be a Christian. But godliness could be established there if there were churches that were like households or extended families. In the increasingly hostile environment of our culture such churches are needed if godliness is to be established and to flourish. Churches are needed in which believers relate to one another as family. Churches are needed in which believers are deeply committed to one another as children of our heavenly Father and as brothers and sisters united together in Jesus Christ. In becoming such churches hospitality plays a vital role as Christians, together as congregations and as families and individuals, share not only food and shelter, but also their lives with one another and with strangers.

2. To establish godliness in the world *leaders* are needed

In order to put in order what Paul had left behind after his mission, Titus is to 'appoint elders in every town' (v. 1). These elders are called 'overseers' in verse 7. Elders and overseers are the same office of leadership in the local church. An overseer is not, as some understand it, a bishop who is over the other elders either in one church or an area, but rather is one of the elders whose responsibility is to lead the local church. This means that ideally there should be a plurality of elders in every local church. Together they are the pastors or shepherds of the church. As such they are together to direct, instruct and protect the church. One or more of the elders or overseers may have a primary ministry of public preaching and teaching, but those who do are equally elders with the other elders. While the first leaders of churches in the New Testament were, like the churches on Crete, appointed by the apostles or their delegates like Titus, the fact that Paul outlines their qualifications indicates that today churches are to recognise leaders and appoint them to their office in the church.

What, then, are the qualifications for leaders in the local church? First, they must be *godly* men. In verses 6–8 Paul lists various godly characteristics of a man who is being appointed to lead the church. Twice Paul says that he must be 'blameless'. Being blameless doesn't mean that the leader must be perfect. The idea of blamelessness is that the leader is to have a good reputation inside and outside the church so that he cannot be accused of any wrongdoing. Such blamelessness is to be particularly evident in his marriage and family life. He is to be 'faithful to his wife'. Literally, he is to be a 'one woman man'. If married, a leader must be married only to one woman and must be sexually faithful to her. Implied here is that he is the Christ-like husband described by Paul in Ephesians 5:25–32.

Not only so, but the leader's children are to 'believe' and not be 'open to the charge of being wild and disobedient'. Does that mean that if a man's children are not professing Christians, he cannot be an elder or if he is one, he must resign? I don't think so. The word 'believe' can also be translated 'trustworthy', as in the NIV footnote, and I think that better fits the context here. What Paul is saying is that the trustworthiness and general good behaviour of a man's children is evidence that he knows how to manage his household and is therefore qualified to manage the church. How well a man brings up his children is no guarantee that they will believe in Jesus for salvation, but while they are under his authority in the home they should not be known for their rebelliousness even if like all children they sometimes misbehave and get into trouble. The point Paul is making is that a man's marriage and family life testify to his godly character.

Then in verse 7 Paul lists five negative characteristics where an elder must be exemplary in the way he controls his appetites and passions. *Negatively* an elder is not to be someone who is:

- 'overbearing' – that is, someone who is self-willed, stubborn, domineering and arrogant, rather than being humble in dealing with people. Sadly, in churches as well as in the world, there are all too many such people who 'lord' it over others rather than working with them for their joy as Paul himself did (2 Cor. 1:24).

- 'quick-tempered' – that is, someone given to anger, rather than being gentle in dealing with people. How much damage anger can do in a church! Angry words that are never repented of can destroy relationships and churches.

- 'given to drunkenness' – rather than being temperate if he drinks alcohol. Letting oneself be controlled by substances such as alcohol or drugs is out of bounds for Christians, never mind leaders.

- 'violent' – that is, not a brawler who loves to pick a fight, rather than being a peacemaker among people. Some people love a good bust-up and seem to be always falling out with people. On occasion the anger can turn physical.

What discredit that brings on the gospel and a church in the local community.

- 'pursuing dishonest gain' – that is, someone motivated by greed and enriching himself dishonestly rather than being content with what he has (1 Tim. 6:6–10). Money is indeed a root of all kinds of evil. Along with sex and power (control) it is a real snare to leaders. Elders need to be beyond reproach in their financial dealings inside and outside the church.

Having listed five negative characteristics Paul now lists six positive characteristics of an elder in verse 8. *Positively* an elder is to be:

- 'hospitable' – that is, someone who welcomes people into his home. Hospitality is the secret weapon of the church and elders should be exemplary in showing it to Christians and non-Christians. The hospitable home of an elder is a showcase for the gospel as people are welcomed and the gospel is seen as well as heard.

- 'one who loves what is good' – that is, someone who loves 'whatever is true ... noble ... right ... pure ... lovely ... [and] admirable' as Paul puts it in Philippians 4:8–9. With so much bad in the world, an elder should love the good and encourage it in people and events. Contrary to our natural tendency his conversation should gravitate to the good rather than the bad.

- 'self-controlled' – that is, someone who has himself under control. Gospel-empowered self-control is key to living a godly life as Paul makes clear in this letter (2:1,5,6,12). An elder who is uncontrolled in his life cannot teach others to be self-controlled.

- 'upright' – that is, someone whose life conforms outwardly to God's law. While inwardly an elder must seek to obey God, it is by his outward behaviour that he is seen and judged by people.

- 'holy' – that is, someone who is devoted to God and lives to please him. An elder should be a man who is evidently set apart for God and living accordingly. The early nineteenth century Scottish minister Robert Murray M'Cheyne said that his people's greatest need was his personal holiness. That is true of every elder.

- 'disciplined' – that is, someone who is master of himself.

These six virtues that are to positively characterise an elder, along with the five vices that that they should not be known for, give us a profile of the godly man an elder is to be. Again, he is not to be perfect, but he is to be a godly man who will be an example of godliness to other Christians.

In all that I have been saying it is clear that I believe that elders of local churches should be male. That is a somewhat controversial point and not all readers will agree with me, but it seems to me that the Bible is clear on the matter. In 1 Timothy 2:12 Paul writes that a woman is not to teach or have authority over a man. The principle seems to be that in the household of God, as in the natural household, men are to be the leaders. That doesn't mean that women are inferior to men but rather that in the church as in the human family they have a different and complementary role to men.

As Paul makes clear in this letter (2:4–7) and in other letters there is much women can do to advance the gospel inside and outside the church, from being deacons (Rom. 16:1–2; 1 Tim. 3:8–13) to contending on the front line of evangelism and church planting (Rom. 16:3–7,12–15; Phil. 4:2–3). Much has been written about this matter and much more could be said. My personal view is that women can do everything in the church and outside it except what the Bible says only elders can do and what that means in practice will vary in some degree from culture to culture.

Secondly, as well as being godly men, leaders in the local church are to be *gospel* men. That is, they must 'hold firmly the trustworthy message as it has been taught' (v. 9). The 'trustworthy message' is the gospel that was taught by the apostles. When Paul wrote this letter, the teaching of the apostles was handed down to people directly by him or the other apostles or their associates orally or in written form. Today we have the teaching of the apostles written by the Spirit's inspiration in our Bibles. Elders or overseers of local churches must hold fast to this gospel and not deviate from it. However pleasant a personality someone might have and however gifted he might be, if an elder is not a gospel man he is dangerous. He will be a wolf in sheep's clothing who will destroy the flock, as Paul warned the elders of the church in Ephesus (Acts 20:28–31). Elders must be doctrinally orthodox men. They must be men with a deep heartfelt commitment to the truth of the gospel. Sadly, as history teaches us, when that isn't the case churches will in time depart from the gospel.

Thirdly, a leader in the local church must also be a *gifted* man. That is, he must be able to 'encourage others by sound doctrine and refute those who oppose it' (v. 9). The core ministry of leaders in a local church is to prayerfully preach and teach the Word (Acts 6:2,4). Among the leaders there will be a variety of gifts in this area. As I've said, one or more of the elders will be gifted in public preaching and teaching. Other elders may do that occasionally. All the elders should be gifted in communicating the Word of God in conversations, pastoral counsel, discussions and Bible study.

However, while elders need to be gifted in teaching the Word they do not need to be super-gifted. It is far more important that they are godly gospel men. Of course, we mustn't despise men who are highly gifted, especially in preaching. The church has been greatly blessed in the past as well as in the present with great preachers. Think of Augustine, Martin Luther, John Calvin, George Whitefield, C H Spurgeon, Martyn Lloyd-Jones, John Stott, William Still, Eric Alexander and others. But the best such preachers were godly gospel men, as are many like them today. What matters more than gifting is godliness and a firm commitment to the gospel of grace.

All this needs to be remembered as men are recognised and prepared for leadership in local churches. That process begins by testing them to see if they are gifted in teaching and preaching, evangelism and relating to people as they deal with pastoral and spiritual concerns. Training for ministry can be done 'in-house' or with other like-minded churches. Some men, particularly if they are on track to become ministers or pastors of churches, will benefit from higher level training in a theological college. Some will go even further to more advanced theological training so that they are equipped in various disciplines as the theologians the churches need, both as pastors and educators. The church has benefitted from pastor-theologians such as Jonathan Edwards, Andrew Fuller, Martyn Lloyd-Jones and Timothy Keller as well as theological teachers such as Herman Bavinck, B B Warfield, J I Packer and Roger Nicole. A new generation of such theologians needs to be raised up.

However, it is not only elders of local churches that need to be recognised and prepared for leadership, but others as well at all levels of local church life. Depending on their ministry, men and women need to be trained to teach children, lead small groups, give pastoral counsel, teach the Bible, do evangelism and more. But whoever they are and whatever their ministry it is essential that as well as being gifted they are godly people committed to the gospel.

3. To establish godliness in the world, *teaching* is needed

Whatever else a church does and whatever their particular gifting, the leaders must make sure that the teaching of the gospel is at the heart of its life. Only in that way will godliness be established and flourish wherever a church is located. Christians need to be taught the gospel from the Bible so that they can become godly. But teaching the Word is not merely about imparting information about the contents and doctrines of the Bible. No, teaching the Word is about explaining the message of the Bible to people so that they will understand it and then applying that message to their lives so that they become godly in the way they live. That is what Paul means when he writes that the leaders are to 'encourage others with sound doctrine' (v. 9). Whatever form their teaching takes, elders are to build up Christians with the sound or healthy doctrine of the gospel found in the Bible.

This really cannot be over-emphasised. Teaching or doctrine matters. It is through the teaching of the gospel that we come to faith. In Romans 6:17, Paul reminds the Roman Christians of how they had obeyed from their hearts 'the pattern of teaching that has now claimed your allegiance'. And it is through the teaching of the gospel that we grow in faith and knowledge of Jesus Christ so that we mature as Christians. As Paul said to the Ephesians elders as he bid them farewell: 'Now I commit you to God and the word of his grace, which can build you up and give you an inheritance among all those who are sanctified' (Acts 20:32). Whatever happened in the future, Paul knew that it was the gospel alone that would enable the Ephesian Christians to mature in their faith and, against all the human odds, attain their inheritance.

That was just as true for the Cretan Christians, and it is just as true for Christians today and in every generation. Against all that the world, the flesh and the devil throws at local churches, it is the faithful teaching of the gospel from the Bible and the lives that are transformed as a result that enables them to flourish even in the most hostile environment.

But as well as encouraging believers by the sound doctrine of the gospel the leaders of a church must also 'refute those who oppose it'. Sadly, there are those who oppose the truth. While this opposition to the truth often comes from outside the church, sadly it sometimes comes from inside as well. For various reasons Christians are led away from the truth and into error. When that happens, the elders must seek to protect the church by opposing those seeking to lead her astray by false teaching. Unpopular as this negative side of a teaching ministry is, it is necessary when false teaching is threatening a church. That doesn't mean we should become heresy hunters or that preachers should always be railing against false teachers. But we must be vigilant and when false teaching does appear it must be exposed and opposed. And what that means Paul goes on to explain in verses 10–16 that we will look at in the next chapter.

Here, then, is how godliness is to be established, be it in first century Crete or twenty-first century London, in Rome or Lusaka, Yangon or Boston, or anywhere else at any time. Remember that godliness is devotion to God actively expressed in a good life empowered by the gospel. Such godliness is the big thing that must be our purpose as churches and as Christians. To establish such godliness three things are needed: churches, leaders and teaching. If we are serious about godliness, we will take these three things seriously. We will pray and work to make sure that our churches have godly, gifted gospel men as elders and overseers and that the preaching and teaching of the gospel is at the heart of everything we do. But we will also prayerfully do all we can to see other churches than our own flourishing, in this country and around the world, and weaker churches being strengthened and new churches being started. Led by godly, gifted gospel men these churches will have at their heart faithful ministries of preaching and teaching of the Word that encourage Christians with sound doctrine and refute those who oppose it. That is how godliness gains a beachhead in the world.

Questions for discussion

1. Why do local churches matter in nurturing godliness and what kind of churches must they be?

2. What are the qualifications for leadership (elders) in local churches and why is godly character so essential? Spend time reflecting on each of these qualifications.

3. Discuss the positive and negative aspects of the teaching ministry of elders.

4. What is the best way for local church leaders to be trained?

5. Why is orthodox theology so important in training elders and the exercise of their ministry?

Chapter 3

False teachers endanger godliness and must be opposed (Titus 1:10-16)

There is a great danger facing the church today. Contrary to what some people may think, that danger is not primarily persecution even though more Christians are being persecuted today than ever in history. Of course, persecution is a danger. Low level persecution in the form of hostility can wear down Christians and churches and high-level persecution that is violent can involve great suffering and even death. Around the world there are many Christians who face high level persecution every day. But often where there is such persecution the church grows as more people become Christians. This doesn't always happen, and we should be careful not to romanticise persecution. But there is some truth in the saying of the early church father Tertullian that the blood of the martyrs is the seed of the church.

But whatever happens, persecution is not the greatest danger facing the church. Nor are the great dangers the various political and cultural forces arrayed against orthodox Christianity. For example, there's a lot of talk in the

United Kingdom and other western nations about the soft totalitarianism of 'cultural Marxism' or the woke revolution. This is the attempt by socially and culturally 'progressive' groups in politics, the media, education and so on to force people to conform to an agenda in which everything is seen in terms of oppression and group identity.

One aspect of this is that everyone can determine their own identity especially when it comes to sexuality and gender. There is a great danger in all this for the church and in the future the pressures will get much worse. Nevertheless, I don't think that or anything similar is the greatest danger facing the church in Europe today.

Other dangers could be mentioned, but the great danger I have in mind is false teaching. Over and over in the New Testament we are warned of the danger of false teaching. The majority of letters in the New Testament deal in some way with its danger. The passage that we're looking at in this chapter is one example of this. In describing the qualifications of elders to be appointed in the churches on Crete, Paul has mentioned that not only must they be able to encourage believers with sound doctrine, but they must also be able to 'refute those who oppose it' (v. 9). That is, they must be able to deal with the danger of false teaching by refuting the false teachers themselves. In verses 10–16 Paul goes on to describe these false teachers.

Christians today need to take seriously what Paul writes here. I admit that at first this is not the most appealing passage. It all sounds rather negative. But by definition a danger is negative, and we need to hear the warning against it if we want to be safe. And what makes false teaching so dangerous is that it undermines and attacks the gospel with the result that Christian living is destabilised and Christian witness is compromised. That happens because false teaching finds a reception in the hearts of people, whether those who teach it or those who accept it. For false teaching is not merely an intellectual issue. The problem is not merely that there are some wrong ideas that need to be corrected. Rather, the problem is that in their hearts something is wrong spiritually with people with the result that they start to believe it and behave accordingly.

So, to help us as Christians and as churches to avoid the danger of false teaching I want us to look at the marks of a false teacher. What Paul writes here may not apply exactly to every false teacher everywhere and in every time, but there is a general picture here painted in broad strokes that helps us to identity those who would lead Christians astray with a false gospel. Identifying the marks of a false teacher will help us to see the marks of a true teacher – the true teachers that should be the leaders of churches where godliness is being nurtured.

Who were these false teachers in Crete? This passage gives us several clues. They belonged to 'the circumcision group' (v. 10.). That identifies these false teachers as Jewish. They were probably Jews who professed to follow Jesus but put a big emphasis on circumcision. Basically, they said that Gentile Christians had to become Jews in order to be saved. This was a big problem in the early church as the book of Acts, as well as Paul's letter to the Galatians, bear witness. But this group on Crete was also into 'Jewish myths' and 'merely human commands' (v. 14). There seemed to be a fascination with mystical fables of a Jewish nature. Paul warned Timothy about this in 1 Timothy 1:3–4,

> As I urged you when I went into Macedonia, stay there in Ephesus so that you may command certain people not to teach false doctrines any longer or to devote themselves to myths and endless genealogies. Such things promote controversial speculations rather than advancing God's work—which is by faith.

As well as that there were commands that people devised. This is what Paul has in mind in 1 Timothy 4:1–3 when he writes:

> The Spirit clearly says that in later times some will abandon the faith and follow deceiving spirits and things taught by demons. Such teachings come through hypocritical liars, whose consciences have been seared as with a hot iron. They forbid people to marry and order them to abstain from certain foods, which God created to be received with thanksgiving by those who believe and who know the truth.

In Colossians 2:18 he warns about such people:

> Do not let anyone who delights in false humility and the worship of angels disqualify you. Such a person also goes into great detail about what they have seen; they are puffed up with idle notions by their unspiritual mind.

We may not be endangered by exactly that false teaching today, but there is always false teaching in some form that says that salvation is not by faith alone in Jesus Christ. Even 'Christian' teaching can be false, such as liberal theology or the prosperity gospel, endangering Christians and the churches by subtracting from or adding to salvation in Christ alone through faith alone by grace alone. We must be constantly vigilant and on our guard against the danger. Let's turn to the passage and note the characteristics first of a false teacher and then of a true teacher.

The marks of a *false* teacher

How can you tell a false teacher? At first, he or she may not look like one. They are likely to seem pleasant enough and to talk well and to be persuasive. They will probably use biblical words and have what Paul elsewhere calls 'a form of godliness' (2 Tim. 4:5). That is, they will outwardly have the look of being orthodox, maybe by the clothes they wear or the language they use or the credentials they have. However, in reality, as Jesus said, they 'come to you in sheep's clothing, but inwardly are ferocious wolves' (Mt. 7:15). If that is the case how can we identify a false teacher? Here there are seven marks to note.

(1) A false teacher is rebellious
Paul warns Titus that on Crete 'there are many rebellious people' (v. 10) and there are still many today. False teachers are in rebellion against God and his Word. They refuse to submit to the authority of God in Scripture. They do this in different

ways. They may say they believe the Bible to be God's Word, but they twist and distort its meaning. This is what heretical cults such as the Jehovah's Witnesses do or what false teachers like Prosperity Gospel teachers do. The former, among other things, deny the deity of the Lord Jesus and the latter, while formally orthodox on essential belief, distort the gospel with a largely materialistic understanding of what it means for God to bless his people.

Or false teachers may say that while they revere the Bible it is not infallible and contains errors of various kinds. This is what older theological liberals do so that they can dismiss what the Bible clearly teaches and understand Christianity in a naturalistic way with no room for the supernatural. Newer versions of liberalism may be more open to the supernatural but still reject the authority of the Bible and deny its infallibility, especially when it comes to sexual morality. Or false teachers like the Mormons and others can simply listen more to what they claim to be new revelations from God.

(2) A false teacher is deceptive

The false teachers were 'full of meaningless talk and deception' (v. 10). Deception characterised 'the circumcision group', but it is true of all false teachers. They teach what is false even as they claim it is true. Deceived themselves, they seek to deceive others (2 Tim. 3:13). They don't speak the truth. They are like the false prophets condemned by Jeremiah:

> They dress the wound of my people
> as though it were not serious.

'Peace, peace,' they say,
when there is no peace (8:11).

Without a true word from God, they say that everything is okay when it is not and people are facing his judgment. As Jeremiah says in 23:16–18,

This is what the LORD Almighty says:

"Do not listen to what the prophets are prophesying to you;
they fill you with false hopes.
They speak visions from their own minds,
not from the mouth of the LORD.
They keep saying to those who despise me,
'The LORD says: You will have peace.'
And to all who follow the stubbornness of their hearts
they say, 'No harm will come to you.'
But which of them has stood in the council of the LORD
to see or to hear his word?
Who has listened and heard his word?

False teachers twist the words of the Bible to say things they don't mean and to tell people what they want to hear (2 Tim. 4:3). In the context of Crete, circumcision was so attractive because it appealed to sinful human pride and the desire to contribute something to salvation. Today it might be something like attending church or giving to charity or anything else we might trust, instead of trusting in Christ alone for salvation.

(3) A false teacher is destructive

The false teachers on Crete needed to be 'silenced' or muzzled like wild beasts because they were 'disrupting [or destroying] whole households by teaching things they ought not to teach' (v. 11). They seem to have gone around to homes with the intention of deliberately leading families astray. Or it could be that the households led astray were house churches. Whatever the case, the impact was destructive of spiritual life. That continues to be the case today, seen for example in the way false teachers are directly attacking family life in churches by condoning same sex marriage and transgenderism.

(4) A false teacher is dishonest

The false teachers do what they do 'for the sake of dishonest gain' (v. 11). Paul has in mind the false teachers who went around peddling their teaching for profit like dodgy door-to-door salesmen (2 Cor. 3:17). Today false teachers are unlikely to do that in a country like the UK. But they might earn their salary as ministers in denominations, churches or institutions whose confessions or statements of faith they deny in their teaching. Or in the case of Prosperity Gospel teachers, they may make themselves rich by fleecing gullible followers. Sadly, it must be said that a love of money corrupts some people so that they dishonestly use religion to make themselves rich.

(5) A false teacher is worldly

In verses 12–13 Paul writes: 'One of Crete's own prophets has said it: "Cretans are always liars, evil brutes, lazy gluttons." This

saying is true. Therefore rebuke them sharply, so that they will
be sound in the faith'. Here Paul quotes a Cretan poet named
Epimenides who lived about 600 BC. He had some pretty
unflattering things to say about his own people. Not only were
they 'liars, evil brutes and lazy gluttons' but in another place he
said that the absence of wild beasts on Crete was made up for
by the people.

From other sources we know that the Cretans had a bad
reputation in the ancient world. To 'Cretanize' was a common
expression for lying. Why does Paul quote this pagan Greek
philosopher? He does so to make the point that the false
teachers on Crete conformed to their culture. In other words,
they were worldly. For sure, what Epimenides said about
the Cretans was a stereotype and not all Cretans were as he
describes them. But that was their reputation, and the false
teachers are conforming to it by being deceptive, destructive
and dishonest.

Today the same thing happens with false teachers. They
conform to all the worst trends of their own culture and follow
the world rather than faithfully engaging it with the gospel.
Every culture has good and bad aspects and false teachers
and their teaching often reflect the bad aspects. They do so
because, rather than being transformed by the renewal of their
minds through the gospel, they let themselves be conformed
to the world as it is manifest in their native culture. That's why
people are so open to their false teaching. The false teachers
are teaching what seems normal and makes people feel

comfortable but leaves the idols of their culture untouched. That happens in Britain as much as anywhere else.

(6) A false teacher is impure

In verse 15 Paul writes: 'To the pure, all things are pure, but to those who are corrupted and do not believe, nothing is pure. In fact, both their minds and consciences are corrupted'. Why do false teachers teach what they do? It is because they are impure in their hearts. Their minds and consciences are corrupted. Their thinking and how they judge what they do has been corrupted by their sin. As a result, their teaching is like a fountain contaminated with poison. Jesus made this point when he said that it is not what enters us that makes us unclean but our hearts from which unclean things come (Mk. 7:20–23). It is from the overflow of the heart that the tongue speaks and if the heart is bad what a person says will be bad.

(7) A false teacher is hypocritical

Obviously, the false teachers 'claim to know God' (v. 16). How could they do otherwise as teachers of what they understand to be Christianity? But the truth is that they are hypocrites since 'by their actions they deny him'. By their false teaching and by their ungodly lifestyle they deny the God they claim to know. The big problem of the false teachers is that they do not know the God they claim to know and talk about. In other words, they are not Christians whatever they claim. The evidence is in their actions which are contrary to genuine Christianity.

For that reason, Paul concludes the false teaches 'are detestable, disobedient and unfit for doing anything good'. That's strong language, although mild for Paul. In Philippians 3:2 he calls false teachers dogs and mutilators of the flesh. The point is that false teaching is a deadly serious matter and those who teach a false gospel are enemies of the truth. They cause spiritual havoc and are a deadly danger to Christians and the church.

What can be done about the false teachers? An attempt should be made to rescue them from their folly. In verse 13 Paul urges Titus to 'rebuke them sharply, so that they will be sound in faith'. On this matter Titus mustn't pussy-foot about and neither must we. False teachers must be confronted with the sin of what they are teaching with the aim that they would repent and come to have a healthy faith in Christ. Paul made much the same point to Timothy:

> Opponents must be gently instructed, in the hope that God will grant them repentance leading them to a knowledge of the truth, and that they will come to their senses and escape from the trap of the devil, who has taken them captive to do his will. (2 Tim. 2:25–26)

But what happens if the false teachers don't repent? Then, if they are members of the church, they must be removed from its membership. As Paul writes in 3:10–11,

Warn a divisive person once, and then warn them a second time. After that, have nothing to do with them. You may be sure that such people are warped and sinful; they are self-condemned.

This is not a pleasant business, but it is necessary for the good of the church. Sadly, it was a failure to exercise church discipline in relation to false teaching that contributed to what C H Spurgeon called 'the Downgrade' in the Nonconformist churches in the late nineteenth century and it is still happening today. Spurgeon said:

The first step astray is a want of adequate faith in the divine inspiration of the sacred Scriptures. All the while a man bows to the authority of God's Word, he will not entertain any sentiment contrary to its teaching. "To the law and to the testimony," is his appeal concerning every doctrine. He esteems that holy Book, concerning all things, to be right, and therefore he hates every false way. But let a man question, or entertain low views of the inspiration and authority of the Bible, and he is without chart to guide him, and without anchor to hold him.[1]

We must be on our guard against false teachers and do what is necessary to protect the churches.

The marks of a *true* teacher

If a false teacher is such a danger to the church what are the marks of a true teacher who will do a church good? They will be the opposite of those of a false teacher. So, although not mentioned explicitly in the passage let's consider what a true teacher is like.

(1) A true teacher is submissive

Unlike a rebellious false teacher, a true teacher will gladly submit to God and his Word. He will be a man under authority. He will be, in the words of John Stott, 'a Bible man'. That will manifest itself in his commitment to preaching from the Bible. Rather than impose his views on the Bible or spouting his own ideas or those of others, a true teacher will seek to the best of his ability to humbly expound what God has revealed in the words of inspired Scripture. Not only so, but he will seek to shape his whole ministry as well as his life by the Word of God.

(2) A true teacher is truthful

Unlike a deceptive false teacher, a true teacher will seek to be truthful in all he says. With Paul in 2 Corinthians 4:2 he will say,

> Rather, we have renounced secret and shameful ways; we do not use deception, nor do we distort the word of God. On the contrary, by setting for the truth plainly we commend ourselves to everyone's conscience in the sight of God.

There is no place for deception in Christian ministry. A true teacher doesn't have to resort to clever tricks but can simply trust God to work by his Word. The words of Malachi 2:6 should be said of him: 'True instruction was in his mouth and nothing false was found on his lips. He walked with me in peace and uprightness and turned many from sin'. Those words (in the language of the Authorized Version) are found on the memorial to Jonathan Edwards in Northampton, Massachusetts and should sum up the ministry of every pastor as they did that of Edwards.

So too should the words of the next verse, Malachi 2:7, 'For the lips of the priest ought to preserve knowledge, because he is a messenger of the LORD Almighty and people seek instruction from his mouth'. Under the new covenant no Christian is a priest in the same sense as the old covenant priesthood. Nevertheless, new covenant pastors, like old covenant priests, teach the people of God and as they do so faithfully, God's people will hear his voice.

(3) A true teacher is constructive

Unlike a destructive false teacher, a true teacher seeks to build believers up in the faith. His 'sound doctrine' (v. 9) will be spiritually healthy and help to nurture godliness and stronger faith in Christians. Households, whether they are families or local churches, won't be disrupted and destroyed but built up so that they can flourish in a world that is hostile to godliness.

(4) A true teacher is honest

Unlike a dishonest false teacher, the true teacher will not be trying to make money out of his teaching. For sure he is likely to be paid by his church, but money should not be his motivation. When it comes to money his dealings will be honest and above board. Of course, as with sex and power so with money there is always temptation, but by God's grace it must and can be resisted and guarded against. And the true teacher certainly will not try to manipulate people emotionally and spiritually in order to get their money. With Paul he should be able to say, as he puts it in 1 Thessalonians 2:5 – 'You know that we never used flattery, nor did we put on a mask to cover up greed – God is our witness'. Rather than being greedy for money a true teacher should trust God and be content with what he provides.

(5) A true teacher is godly

Unlike a worldly false teacher, a true teacher seeks not to be conformed to this world, but to be transformed as his mind is renewed by the gospel (Rom. 12:1-2). In other words, he seeks to become increasingly godly in the way Paul describes in verses 5-9. Of course, he lives in this world and as such can't help but be influenced by it to some degree. It is particularly difficult to see the bad aspects of the culture one is brought up in; we can easily have blind spots for the idols of our culture. That is why we must let the Bible shape our thinking so that we are not captured by our culture and conformed to it, but rather liberated from it so that we can serve it with the gospel. True teachers will always be counter-cultural in their lifestyle even as they connect with the dominant culture.

(6) A true teacher is pure

Unlike an impure false teacher, a true teacher has a heart that has been purified by God's grace. That doesn't mean he is perfect, but it does mean that his heart has been cleansed by the Holy Spirit. That happened because by his death on the cross Jesus gave himself to redeem us and 'to purify for himself a people who are his very own, eager to do what is good' (2:14). And because, like every believer, a true teacher has been cleansed by the blood of Jesus, for him 'all things are pure' (v. 15). Forgiven by God and having a pure heart means he can enjoy God's good creation with a good conscience and a mind cleansed and enlightened with the truth of the gospel.

(7) A true teacher is sincere

Unlike a hypocritical false teacher, a true teacher confirms that he really knows God by his actions. There is a sincerity about what he teaches and how he lives that reveals that he genuinely knows the God he is talking about. Again, he is not perfect and is always repenting of sin, but you know that this guy isn't a fake as he lives out his life before God. Therefore, far from being detestable, disobedient and unfit for doing anything good, he is honourable, obedient and fit for doing everything good.

However, it must be said that there are some people whose teaching is correct but who are hypocrites because of the way they live. And sadly, there are all too many examples of this, past and present. Christian leaders who were or are respected and followed by many, turn out to have been living a lie. How they were living was contrary to the Word of God. In some cases it turns out that the leader may never have been a believer in the first place, however gifted he may have been. But some of these people seem to be genuine believers as far as we can judge. When that is the case, it is a reminder that even with believers the heart remains deceitful, corrupt and beyond understanding (Jer. 17:9). How easy it is to deceive ourselves when we sin. Therefore, not only true teachers and leaders, but everyone who is a Christian must guard his or her heart and never stop fighting sin in the power of the Spirit.

Here, then, is a profile of a true teacher in contrast to a false teacher. True teachers like this should be appointed as elders or overseers in local churches, particularly as the lead elders or overseers, that is, the ministers or pastors.[2] True teachers like this should be training for gospel ministry in seminaries and theological colleges and in other ways. True teachers like this who are in leadership positions need to be sustained spiritually as well as intellectually so that they remain true to the faith and live lives of godly integrity.

So, while we must be vigilant and on our guard against false teachers and exercise church discipline when necessary, we must also positively do all we can as Christians and churches to make sure that our particular churches and other churches are being led by true teachers and not by false teachers. What does that mean practically? Among other things it means that each of us remains faithful to the gospel and that we love to hear it taught from the Bible. It means that each of us is faithful in prayer for our church and other churches and for those who lead them and teach the people of God. It means that each of us will encourage true teachers and support them, especially when the world is against them. Then whatever dangers the church faces in this world there is nothing to fear.

Questions for discussion

1. Why is false teaching so dangerous to the churches?

2. What are some of the forms of false teaching that threaten evangelical churches today?

3. Discuss the characteristics of false teachers and then true teachers.

4. How must churches deal with false teaching and why do they often not?

5. What is the best remedy for false teaching?

Godly lifestyle

Chapter 4

Godliness is expressed in a lifestyle that is shaped by the gospel and commends it (Titus 2:1–10)

A few miles from where I live in London is Stamford Hill which is home to one of the largest Hasidic or Haredi Jewish populations in the world. Hasidic Jews are the very orthodox Jews who are noted for the distinctive way they dress and for their intense community life. If you spend any time in Stamford Hill you can't miss seeing Hasidic Jews. The men in particular are notable by their forelocks, velvet or fur-trimmed hats, long gabardine coats and in some cases white stockings and breeches. The clothing owes its origins to the way people dressed in eighteenth and nineteenth century eastern Europe, from where many Jews in this country came to escape persecution. Today that clothing is one of the many traditions that distinguish Hasidic Jews from other people in London. And all this is rooted in their orthodox Jewish faith. In short, Hasidic Jews have a very distinctive lifestyle that expresses who they are and what they believe and value most.

To what extent are evangelical Christians notable for their lifestyle as Christians? Everyone has a lifestyle. A lifestyle is simply the way a person or group of people lives, as shaped by the things they believe and value as most important. Today people are probably more conscious of their lifestyle than ever, at least in a superficial way. Almost every newspaper has a lifestyle section where there are articles on health, fashion, fitness, food, travel, home decor and much more. There are magazines devoted specifically to any one of those areas. Go on the internet and you can't escape people and organisations trying to influence your lifestyle. In fact, lifestyle influencers have become a big phenomenon on social media outlets such as Instagram and TikTok, some with millions of followers. If you really want to and can afford it, you can hire a lifestyle coach who can help sort out your life in some way. But behind all this are the things in the world that influence what people believe and value as most important so that they live in the way they do. None of us is immune to that. Each of us lives as we do because of what we believe and value as most important in life. Each of us has a lifestyle. It may not be that of a Hasidic Jew or a rich footballer and his family profiled in a celebrity magazine, but it is just as much a lifestyle.

The question for each of us is this: what is my lifestyle or way of life because of what I believe and value as most important? Of course, as Christians we believe in what the Bible tells us about God, his creation and about his plan of salvation in Jesus

Christ. Most of us reading this book who are Christians would say that our relationship with God through Jesus Christ is the most important thing in our lives. But how much does that shape our lifestyle or the way we live? How distinctively do we live as Christians? Are we identified as Christians by non-Christians not so much by how we dress or what we eat or don't eat or the like, but by our Jesus-like character and how that is seen in the way we live? Sadly, all too often we are not all that different from non-Christians. To some extent that is to be expected since we share many things with other people as human beings, and in Europe cultures are still deeply influenced by Christianity. Nevertheless, if we are Christians there should be something distinctive about our lifestyle because of what we believe and value most as Christians.

Having warned the young believers on Crete about false teachers who were all too much conformed to the worst aspects of Cretan culture, Paul now turns to encourage them to live distinctively as Christians. And what is to distinguish them is their godly lifestyle. Having come to trust in Jesus for salvation, the Cretan believers are to live in a way shaped by what they now believe and value as most important. That same is to be true of us as Christians today. Believing in Jesus for salvation, that is, being a Christian, is not to be merely one aspect of our lives that we fit in with all the other aspects. Being a Christian must shape everything about us and not least our lifestyle. At their best that has been the case with Christians in the past. In the early church, Christians were known for their lifestyle that was constantly running up against that of their pagan neighbours.

In the seventeenth century the Puritans were known for a notably godly lifestyle that was often ridiculed and opposed. Of course, these Christians were not perfect, and some were far from consistent in the way they lived and in some cases were hypocrites – in a fallen world that has been and always will be the case. Nevertheless, while we won't get it perfectly right, we should strive as Christians to have a godly lifestyle that is shaped by what we believe and value as most important. And as the influence of Christianity on our culture decreases this is an even more urgent priority for us as Christians. We must not be conformed to the world but be transformed by the renewing of our minds so that there is a godly lifestyle that marks us out individually and together as Christians.

A godly lifestyle is necessary

Paul's instruction to Titus is that he 'must teach what is appropriate to sound doctrine' (v. 1). The 'sound doctrine' or teaching is the gospel. It is the 'teaching about God our Saviour' that Paul mentions in verse 10 and summarises so beautifully in verses 11–14. What is it that is so 'appropriate to sound doctrine' that Titus is to teach? It is the godly lifestyle Paul outlines in verses 2–10. It is imperative that Titus teaches these things as he encourages and rebukes people with all authority (verse 15).

Why is it that Paul puts such a big emphasis on this? It is because for him the doctrine of the gospel must be expressed in the way people who believe in Jesus live their everyday lives. Doctrine is not just some ideas that people believe, however correct, that are preached on Sunday but have no bearing on the rest of the week and indeed on Sunday itself as well as the wider world. No, doctrine is to be seen in the way we live. False doctrine has bad consequences and true doctrine has good consequences, or at least it should. Paul is crystal clear, in this letter and others he wrote, as is the whole New Testament, that the doctrine of the gospel is to have a positive effect on the way Christians live. Being a Christian should really make a difference to the way we live. If it doesn't, something is wrong.

That must be how it is with Christians today. Sadly, some Christians can put a big emphasis on correct doctrine or theology, but it doesn't affect their lives in any noticeable way. As Paul writes in 1 Corinthians 8, their knowledge puffs them up with pride but they fail to build other people up with love. That can be a real problem with Christians who rightly love the truth of the gospel and the intellectual stimulation of theology. Some reading this book may need to be on their guard in this area. By all means treasure the truth and dig deeply into it, but also remember that doctrine is not an end in itself. Doctrine is about God and his salvation, and it embraces the whole of life. Doctrine is meant to bring change to our lives as the Holy Spirit uses the truth to work in our hearts. In the words of the seventeenth century Puritan theologian William Ames, 'theology is the doctrine or teaching of living to God'.[1] In other words, the purpose of doctrine is that people who believe in Jesus become godly in their lifestyle. We must make sure that our doctrine is practical.

But it is also necessary to make sure that our practice is doctrinal. What do I mean by that? I mean that how we live as Christians must be rooted in the doctrine of the gospel. If for some Christians doctrine is too disconnected from life, for other Christians the doctrine of the gospel seems to mean little to how they think about living in the world. For sure they believe the gospel, but that is thought of as the ABC of conversion and not as what motivates and shapes their lives. They are very practical but often what they do is not guided by the Word of God. They are up to speed with the latest wisdom of the world in some area such as management theory or psychology, but it is not really the message of the Bible that is shaping their thinking. That too can be a danger and is perhaps a greater one. In living as Christians, individually as well as in the life of the church, we must make sure that the doctrine of the gospel is shaping both what we think and what we do. For sure there is much wisdom in the world that we can use with discernment, but first and foremost we must submit to God and his Word so that the doctrine of the gospel is what determines what we believe and value most.

A godly lifestyle is practical

What does a godly lifestyle mean practically? In verses 3–11 Paul describes what it means for Christians to put God's truth to work in their lives. He doesn't mention everything. For that we need to read the rest of the New Testament. What Paul does describe is what he felt needed to be emphasised for the young believers on Crete. But what he describes helps us to understand how the gospel is to shape the way we live.

(1) What a godly lifestyle means practically for older and younger men

Paul begins by addressing 'older men' in the churches in verse 2. The Greek word translated 'older men' suggests that Paul means men we would think of as middle-aged, roughly aged thirty to sixty. He says that godly older men should be characterised by six qualities. The first three were venerated in the Roman culture of Paul's day. Older men are to be, first, *temperate*. That is, they should be moderate and sober-minded in their habits and not go to extremes. How easy it is to lose our heads in pursuing our passions, even legitimate ones, be it sports, or politics, or food and drink or whatever. Temperance doesn't mean that Christian men should be bland fence-sitters who never express themselves with passion. But there will be balance, sobriety and moderation in the way they approach life.

Second, older Christian men are to be *worthy of respect*. That is, they should be dignified and honourable in the way they conduct themselves inside and outside the Christian community. Non-Christians as well as Christians should respect a Christian man for his exemplary character, being the kind of man they look up to and even want to be like.

Third, older Christian men should be *self-controlled*. That is, they should be disciplined and in control of themselves like an athlete in training (1 Cor. 9:24–27). If he is to achieve his ambition of winning a prize in a sports event, an athlete must rigorously discipline himself. So it is with a Christian man when it comes to controlling his passions and appetites and living a godly life.

The fourth, fifth and sixth qualities that Paul mentions are distinctively Christian. Older men are to be, fourthly, *sound in faith*. They are to have a spiritually healthy trust in the Lord Jesus that is becoming stronger and more mature. Having become Christians through faith in Jesus, that faith should continue to deepen and mature through life as Christian men advance in years. Often that will involve testing and trials, but through them all Christian men's trust in Jesus should become stronger.

Fifth, older Christian men are to be *sound in love*. That is, they are to increasingly reflect in their relationships the love of Jesus for them and theirs for him. They will be increasingly patient with people, kind to them, not envious of them, not boastful of their own achievements, not dishonouring of others to gain advantage or to do them down, not self-seeking but being selfless, not easily angered but gentle, keeping no record of wrongs but forgiving those who wrong them, not delighting when evil and bad things happen to someone, but rejoicing in the truth, and always seeking to protect people from being hurt in some way, always trusting them until they can't anymore, always hoping for the best in them, and always persevering with difficult people and situations (1 Cor. 13:4–7).

Sixth, older Christian men should be *sound in endurance*. Endurance is the way hope is expressed in the Christian life. Such hope is not wishful thinking or having an optimistic outlook on life, but rather being confident that God will do all that he has promised in his Word. This hope will be seen in the way Christian men persevere and keep going through all the ups and downs of life.

Here in a nutshell is what a godly man is like. If you are a man, is that what you want to be like? Christian men should be the best that a man is, even in the estimation of non-Christians, as someone who is temperate, worth of respect and self-controlled. Everyone respects a man like that. But as Christians, men should also be characterised by healthy faith, love and hope. This is the kind of man every male Christian should strive to become.

And that includes younger Christian men. In much of western culture older men often aspire to be like younger men in their tastes and way of dressing and so on. In most cultures, ancient and modern, it is the opposite. See, for example, those pictures of 1950s football matches when sons wore suits like their fathers. Whatever the case in clothing, when it comes to godliness younger men should aspire to be like older men. In particular, they should aspire to be self-controlled. Skipping down to verse 6 we read: 'Similarly, encourage the young men to be self-controlled'. By 'young men' Paul probably has in mind men in their late teens and twenties. Paul is not saying that the younger men don't need to bother with cultivating the qualities expected in older Christian men; rather he is saying that as they aspire to be such men, they should focus particularly on being self-controlled. Why is that? It is because when younger, it is important to learn to keep a tight rein on passions and appetites. Paul is realistic here. Young men are no different now to back then. Lack of discipline and the ability to control the expression of their emotions, desires and instincts can really mess things up in life, and not only in the short-term but in the long-term as well. Self-control is important in many areas of life, but especially when it comes to sex and the temptations and sins that involves. But more positively, young men need to exercise self-control so that as they get older, they live increasingly godly lives.

And in such godly living, as a man Titus himself was to set an example:

> In everything set them an example by doing what is good. In your teaching show integrity, seriousness and soundness of speech that cannot be condemned, so that those who oppose you may be ashamed because they have nothing bad to say about us (verses 7–8).

Titus was probably in his thirties and was to be a model for younger men in the churches. This would involve his lifestyle as it did for Timothy, as Paul mentions in 1 Timothy 4:12,

> Don't let anyone look down on you because you are young, but set an example for the believers in speech, in conduct, in love, in faith and in purity.

Here in his letter to Titus, Paul's emphasis is on the example Titus gives as a teacher. In his teaching Titus is to show integrity, that is, his *motive* is to be pure, uncorrupted, and consistent with a godly life. There mustn't be a mismatch between what Titus teaches and how he lives. His must walk what he talks. Or put another way, the lifestyle of Titus must exemplify the message he preaches. How many ministries have hit the rocks because of a lack of integrity in some way? Like Timothy, Titus must watch his 'life and doctrine closely' (1 Tim. 4:16) as should every gospel minister and church leader.

Not only so, but the teaching of Titus must be characterised by seriousness. His *manner* is not to be flippant and silly. In preaching and teaching the gospel the most serious and momentous issues are being dealt with and the way that is done must be appropriate. That doesn't mean there is no place for the judicious use of humour or for having a relaxed manner in speaking to people. Certainly, seriousness of manner is not inconsistent with expressing joy in the gospel. Indeed, the greatest preachers of the gospel manifestly delight in Christ. But preachers and teachers must remember that they speak before God to people about their eternal salvation.

And there must also be soundness of speech, that is, the matter of what Titus preached and taught must be the doctrinally sound and spiritually healthy truth of the gospel, and so it must be for every preacher and teacher. Preaching and teaching what does not accord with the truth of the gospel is at best like junk food and at worst is poison that destroys spiritual health and can lead to death. No, preaching should produce spiritually healthy Christians.

What was to be true for Titus is to be true for every gospel minister. When that is the case even those who oppose them and the gospel will 'be ashamed because they have nothing bad to say about us'. We expect unbelievers to oppose the message of the gospel, but they should find it impossible to impugn the

85

character of those who preach it because it is exemplified in their godly character. Whether younger or older, that is the example pastors should set not only for younger men but for everyone in the church.

(2) What a godly lifestyle means practically for older and younger women

No doubt the qualities to be seen in older and younger men are to also be seen in older and younger women. All that Paul said should be true of Christian men should also be true of Christian women. That is suggested by the word 'Likewise' in verse 3. However, there are specific issues possibly related to the circumstances on Crete that Paul wants to address:

> Likewise, teach the older women to be reverent in the way they live, not to be slanderers or addicted to much wine, but to teach what is good. Then they can urge the younger women to love their husbands and children, to be self-controlled and pure, to be busy at home, to be kind, and to be subject to their husbands, so that no one will malign the word of God (verses 3–5).

The lifestyle of older women is to be characterised by reverence. The Greek word translated 'reverent in the way they live' was used to speak of priestesses in a pagan shrine or temple. For Christian women that means that they are to behave as people who live consciously in the presence of God. Very specifically that means older women are not to be 'slanderers' or malicious gossips. It also means that they are not to be 'addicted to much wine'. In the Roman world there was a well-known problem of alcoholism among wealthier women. Perhaps we can update what Paul writes here to not indulging in online verbal abuse or getting addicted to recreational drugs and opioids, although old-fashioned slander and alcoholism are very much still with us and men can be just as guilty. The point is older women, like older men, are to be godly in their lifestyle.

And not only are older women to be godly in their lifestyle, but they are to teach younger women to be the same. In particular, older women are to teach younger women to be godly wives and mothers. Younger women are to follow the example of older women in loving their husbands and children, being self-controlled and morally pure, being busy at home and being kind and good to people as they accept the leadership of their husbands in their marriage and family. Throughout history and across most of today's world this would not be a remarkable thing to say. In western culture today some baulk at what Paul says here and elsewhere. Certainly, it is counter-cultural. But the teaching of the Bible is clear that in marriage and family, as in the church, primary leadership is male. In creation and redemption men and women are equal, but there are different God-ordained roles in the home as well as the church. That doesn't mean men are to be tyrants, as some sinfully are, but rather that they should lead by loving their wives and serving them as Christ loved the church and gave himself for her and continues to care for her (Eph. 5:25–33).

In part, accepting such leadership means that godly wives will be 'busy at home' (v. 5). That might involve fulfilling the honourable vocation of being a homemaker, but not necessarily. What Paul says doesn't mean women cannot work or have a career outside the home. In Paul's day, as throughout much of history and in many parts of the world today, the home for many people would have been a place of work as well as a dwelling. What Paul means is that a wife is responsible for managing the home whatever else she does. As an example of a godly woman who was busy at home, but who also ran a business and did a lot of other things, we need look no further than the wife of noble character in Proverbs 31.

But what about single women? Paul does not mention them, most likely because for various reasons single women were relatively rare in the early church. That is not the case today. In principle what Paul writes here applies to them and to married women without children as much as it does to married mothers. In their particular circumstances, they, like all women, are to be godly in their lifestyle.

In short, whether married or single, whether male or female, whether older or younger, Christians are called by Jesus to be godly in the way they live in this world.

A godly lifestyle is evangelistic

In verses 9–10 Paul addresses slaves, of whom there were many in the early church. Slavery was a massive thing in the ancient world, as it was generally until the nineteenth century. The Romans enslaved people of many nationalities. For some slaves, life was relatively good with some rising to positions of great responsibility and becoming rich and powerful. But for most slaves, the experience of slavery was a demeaning life in which they had no rights and could be – and often were – abused in all sorts of ways. The Bible does not explicitly condemn slavery or demand its abolition, although what it teaches about human beings being created in God's image and about the way God redeems all types of people and unites them in Christ eventually led to slavery disappearing in the Roman Empire. When slavery re-emerged in the Atlantic slave trade, it was gospel-driven people who campaigned successfully for its abolition in the British Empire and the United States and eventually elsewhere.

But why did Jesus or Paul, or other leaders in the church, not condemn slavery or advocate its abolition? They most probably did not for the simple reason that to do so would have provoked the wrath of the Roman imperial authorities on the fledgling Christian movement. It would have been like Christians in the former Soviet Union publicly condemning Communism. But what Paul and others did was to undermine the foundations of the institution of slavery with the gospel so that in time it became unthinkable. The short letter of Paul to Philemon is an example of this. Incidentally, it is the gospel that continues to subvert what is unjust not only in relation to slavery but also racism, abortion, euthanasia, the denial of human rights and much more.

The big point that Paul makes here in verses 9–10 is that the lifestyle of slaves is evangelistic in nature.

> Teach slaves to be subject to their masters in everything, to
> try to please them, not to talk back to them, and not to steal
> from them, but to show that they can be fully trusted, so
> that in every way they will make the teaching about God our
> Saviour attractive.

The godly way in which Christian slaves related to their
masters would commend the gospel to them and others by
making it attractive. By their godly behaviour they would
literally adorn the gospel like the way jewels set in a necklace
bring out the beauty of the person wearing it. And what is
amazing, revolutionary even, is that it is slaves who could do
this! Slaves were despised by Romans and yet it is they whom
Paul specifically mentions as commending the gospel by the
way they adorn it with their godly lifestyle.

And what was true for slaves in the first century is true for
every Christian everywhere, whatever their circumstances. In
a way contrary to human wisdom, God chooses what is foolish
and weak and lowly in the eyes of the world to bring glory to
himself and to advance his kingdom (1 Cor. 1:26–29). It is through
our godly lifestyles that the gospel is made attractive and
adorned. Unbelievers look at us and see how we do our work in
often difficult circumstances, or raise our children, or relate to
our spouses, or bear with suffering, or care for one another in
the church and for people outside it, or simply live in an often-
hostile world. In these and a myriad of other ways we make 'the
teaching of God our Saviour' attractive. Of course, as we have
opportunities we will speak of Jesus and the way of salvation.
Evangelism requires that the gospel be verbally communicated

in some form. But evangelism also requires lives that commend the gospel we communicate. If we are known as Christians, the godliness of our lifestyle should be evangelistic in commending the gospel to unbelievers. Unbelievers should look at how we live and think to themselves that if the gospel can do that then there must be something to it.

One of the most important areas of life where this can happen is in work. Work for some people is satisfying and enjoyable but for others it is boring, tiring or difficult. Rather than jumping out of bed with excitement on Monday morning they can't wait until Friday and the weekend. But whatever our experience of work, as Christians in this fallen world we believe that God made us to work as well as wanting us to rest at least for a day a week. Made in his image, even the most ordinary work gives us dignity as human beings. What is work? Broadly it covers everything we agree to do to fulfil certain duties whether that is in at home or in a workplace, part-time or full-time, paid or unpaid or as an employee or employer. In principle what Paul says to slaves he says to everyone who has a job of some kind to do. While there are good reasons why we might not work for a living – illness, lack of work, retirement and so on – if we can, we should work and not be idle (1 Thes. 5:14; 2 Thes. 3:6–10).

If we work as employees we are to 'be subject to' – accept the authority of our employers – and 'to try to please them' in the way we do our work and conduct ourselves. Negatively that involves not talking back to them or being disrespectful, and positively being honest and trustworthy (2:9–10). In other words, godliness means that as Christians we should be the best workers not in an obsequious way but simply because we want to do good. In writing similarly to the Ephesians Paul says that as workers we are to do our work well even when not being observed (or facing an appraisal) and 'to serve wholeheartedly as if ... serving the Lord' (Eph. 6:5-8; Col. 3:22-25) and not merely because we have a contract.

But Christian employers or managers are also responsible for treating those working under them well and particularly ensuring that they are provided for and are paid a fair wage (Eph. 6:9; Col. 4:1; Jas. 5:4). Sadly, that has not always been the case. Reflecting bad aspects of their cultures, Christian bosses have sometimes treated those working for them unjustly. And some, because of temperament or other reasons, have been domineering and tyrannical. That should not be the case with Christian bosses who want to do good.

But whoever we are – older or younger, men or women, employees or bosses – we are to make the gospel attractive to people evangelistically because of the difference for good it makes to our lives. The gospel made a difference to slaves and other believers in the most unlikely and hostile environment in first century Crete. The gospel continues to make a difference as it changes people in whose lives its power is unleashed. The godly lifestyle described here and elsewhere in the Bible is not the result of people getting their act together and making something of their lives as self-help philosophies teach. No, it is the result of the life-changing power of God's grace that has appeared in Jesus. In the next chapter we will look at Paul's wonderful summary of this gospel in verses 11–14. If you are a Christian, it is that gospel that has changed you and continues to do so. That is what makes a godly lifestyle possible. In yourself a godly lifestyle is impossible, but if you trust in Jesus and are indwelt by his Spirit you will be 'eager to do what is good' (2:14). And because that happens to many who believe in Jesus, not only are individuals changed for good, but communities and societies become better as well. What really changes the world for the better is not primarily what happens in centres of political, economic and cultural power, but what happens in the lives of people who by God's grace are becoming more godly in their lifestyle.

In his wonderful commentary on the Pastoral Letters of Paul, the late Thomas Oden made this perceptive observation on the verses we have been looking at:

> Some would argue that it would do little good to begin in Crete, of all places, with the tiniest bits of behaviour and try to reshape the world towards godliness from the ground up. It might seem at first that the pastoral effort was too microscopic, inordinately micromanaged, and that systemic, institutional, or political evils might better have first been addressed. Yet this is just the point most misunderstood by "systemic" reformers who have not adequately grasped the Apostle's way of transformation: only by descending to reshape social existence beginning with the smallest, least conspicuous matters of daily social conduct is the society changed. This has longer, surer consequences than legislative or ideological posturing.[2]

The gospel transformation that is godliness gives hope to every pastor, evangelist, youth worker, missionary or anyone else who is applying the gospel on the micro-level of the lives of ordinary people. So often, not much seems to be happening and what is happening seems so inconsequential. But what Paul told Titus, and through him what the Holy Spirit tells us, is that what really changes lives and the world is micro-level gospel ministry in places like Crete and indeed your church.

The challenge for us, then, is to be godly in our lifestyle because of the transforming power of the gospel. Like those Hasidic Jews in Stamford Hill, we should be notable because of our lifestyle. But what should make us notable should not so much be something like our clothing, but rather our character and the way we live because of the gospel. Is the gospel changing your lifestyle? Would it be any different if you were not a Christian? Is your lifestyle more influenced by the world or the Word? Living in the kind of world we do, nurturing a godly lifestyle is not easy. Like a garden it must be given constant attention if it is not to be overgrown with weeds. Prayerfully preach the gospel to yourself every day so that in its power you deal with temptation and sin, and that you not only say no to what is ungodly, but also yes to what is godly and pleasing to God. And as you do, Jesus will give more of his Spirit so that by his grace and from your heart your lifestyle will be increasingly godly.

Questions for discussion

1. In our culture, how distinctive are evangelical Christians because of their lifestyle?

2. Why does commitment to the truth of the gospel necessitate a godly lifestyle?

3. Reflect on your lifestyle as an older or younger man or woman in the light of what Paul writes here. How distinctive is it?

4. Why are role models so important in nurturing godly lifestyles?

5. What is so attractive about a godly lifestyle that it commends the gospel?

6. In addition to application in sermons, in what other ways can godly lifestyles be nurtured among:

   - particular groups (married couples, singles, parents, age groups, etc.)?
   - specific areas (work, use of money, IT, etc.)?

Chapter 5

A godly lifestyle is motivated and empowered by the gospel of God's grace in Jesus Christ (Titus 2:11–14)

There are a lot of people talking and writing about grace today. There is an almost endless stream of books and online material about the grace of God. In many of these things the emphasis is on how God is gracious in accepting people like us as we are and in wanting to do us good. It's all about affirming us and making us feel good about ourselves. In what others say about grace the emphasis is almost all on what happens at conversion with little about how grace must empower the Christian life. But there is a problem with both these approaches: with all the talk about grace there is often little talk about sin. You see, you can't understand grace without understanding sin. It is because we are sinners that God is gracious in saving people like us through the Lord Jesus Christ and changing us to be increasingly like him. It is as we understand how deep our sin is and how much we deserve God's wrath that we begin to understand how deep God's grace is and all that he has done in Jesus Christ to save us and change us.

A person who understood the grace of God more than most people was John Newton who wrote the famous hymn, 'Amazing grace', which is still popular with people with a very loose connection with Christianity, if any. It has been sung on many occasions such as the inauguration of President Biden in 2021 where nothing that was distinctively Christian would have been permitted. The reason that is possible is that the name of Jesus is not mentioned. In Newton's time and place, mention of grace would have been connected by people with Jesus, but sadly that is not the case in many places today. But to really appreciate the hymn and to sing it meaningfully you must understand that it was written out of Newton's own experience as a sinner forgiven by God because of what Christ accomplished by his death on the cross. Newton had been a slave trader and on his own admission committed almost every vile sin that could be committed. But he had been converted by repenting of his sins and trusting in Jesus Christ for salvation. That's why, as he neared death as an old man, he could say: 'Although my memory is failing I remember two things: I am a great sinner and Christ is a great Saviour'. But for Newton, God's grace was not only about being saved from his wrath and the hope of eternal life. For Newton, God's grace was also about being changed as a sinner so that he became more godly. In one of the many letters he wrote to people he said this:

> ... though I am not what I ought to be, nor what I wish to be, nor what I hope to be, I can truly say, I am not what I once

97

was – a slave to sin and Satan; and I can heartily join with the Apostle [Paul], and acknowledge: that by the grace of God I am what I am![1]

It is this life-transforming as well as soul-saving grace that we are thinking about in this passage in Titus. Paul has just outlined in verses 1-10 the godly lifestyle that is appropriate to the sound teaching of the gospel. Here in outline is how Christians should live. But how is such a lifestyle possible? How can sinners like us live in a way appropriate to the gospel we believe? In ourselves we don't have the ability. The reason we can be godly as Christians, however imperfectly, is because of the very gospel by which we are saved. The gospel gives those who believe in Jesus for salvation the motivation and the power to live to please God, that is to be godly. This is what Paul writes in verses 11-14:

For the grace of God has appeared that offers salvation to all people. It teaches us to say "No" to ungodliness and worldly passions, and to live self-controlled, upright and godly lives in this present age, while we wait for the blessed hope— the appearing of the glory of our great God and Saviour, Jesus Christ, who gave himself for us to redeem us from all wickedness and to purify for himself a people that are his very own, eager to do what is good.

What we need to understand is that the gospel is not only about how we begin the Christian life but also about how we continue the Christian life. Motivated and empowered by the gospel we can in some measure become godly. This is in part why Jesus has saved us. For sure he has saved us to live forever with him and his people in the new creation as we glorify him with the Father and the Spirit as the one God. But we are also saved by Jesus to be godly in this world as we live in hope of his return. And it is this amazing grace to sinners like us that we want to think about. And as we do so, I trust that if you are a believer in Jesus you will be motivated and empowered to be godly. Like the early believers on Crete, who with Titus first heard this letter, we need to hear what Paul writes here. As with them we live in a world that is hostile to godliness and need all the help and encouragement we can get. So take the message of this passage to heart. But do so also if you are not a Christian. For what we read here tells you why and how you can be saved and your life changed for good because of the amazing grace of God in Jesus Christ.

The grace of God has appeared for our salvation

The 'For' in verse 11 is very significant – 'For the grace of God has appeared that offers salvation to all people'. What Paul is saying is that the godly lifestyle that he has been writing about – the lifestyle like that of godly slaves that makes 'the teaching of God our Saviour attractive' (v. 10) – is possible because of the appearance of God's grace. Having told us what we must do to be godly as Christians, he now tells us why that is possible. In thinking about godliness or the Christian life we must remember this. If we only think about what we must do, we can easily fall into the trap of legalism and moralism. The Christian life becomes all about conforming to the law of God. Now there's nothing wrong with conforming to the law of God. God wants us to obey his will revealed in the moral law. However, law has no power in itself to change us for good. Law tells us what to do but gives us no power or motivation to obey God. And for many, such legalism or moralism is the default position when the gospel of grace is absent. Sadly, this graceless approach to obeying God characterises far too many religious and morally upright people. At best it produces joyless Christians and at worst proud and hypocritical non-Christians who think they are Christians.

So that we don't fall into this trap and so that we know why we can do what God commands, we must understand the grace of God in the gospel. Paul tells us that this grace 'has appeared'. How has God's grace appeared? It has appeared in the person of Jesus Christ. Jesus is the grace of God incarnate. Do you want to know what grace looks like? Look no further than Jesus. Jesus is the walking, talking grace of God. We see God's grace in the birth of Jesus in Bethlehem, in the life of Jesus doing so much good, in the death of Jesus at Calvary, in the resurrection of Jesus and in his ascension to his Father's throne where he now reigns over all things. Don't think of God's grace as something abstract, but rather as a living person, as Jesus Christ.

And this grace that has appeared in Jesus 'offers salvation to all people'. Grace appeared in Jesus because people like us need to be saved. Saved from what? From the wrath or judgment of God for our sins. As sinful rebels we deserve the wrath of God as the Bible makes abundantly clear. But in Jesus Christ, God himself has graciously come to us in person to save us from his own wrath and judgment. This salvation is literally 'for all men' or 'all people'. That doesn't mean everyone will be saved because the grace of God has appeared in Jesus. The Bible doesn't teach universal salvation for everyone. What Paul means is that salvation is for every kind of person. Salvation is for men and women, for Jews and Gentiles and every kind of ethnic group, for people of all social backgrounds and for people of all ages. For that reason, we must offer this salvation to everyone, not knowing who will accept it and believe in Christ.

How amazing is the grace of God that has appeared in Jesus Christ! But how has this grace actually saved sinners like us? Look at verse 14 – Jesus Christ 'gave himself for us to redeem us from all wickedness and to purify for himself a people that are his very own, eager to do what is good'. The grace of God for our salvation is supremely seen in the death of Jesus on the cross where Jesus 'gave himself for us'. On the cross Jesus willingly offered himself up as the one final sacrifice for our sins. As Jesus himself said, he 'did not come to be served, but to serve, and to give his life as a ransom for many' (Mk. 10:45). Jesus was the ransom or sacrifice that was offered up in the place of sinners. As such he bore the punishment that we deserve and turned away God's wrath. As it is put in the letter to the Hebrews, Jesus 'offered himself unblemished to God' (9:14) and 'was sacrificed once to take away the sins of many' (9:28). Or as the apostle Peter puts it, 'Christ ... suffered once for sins, the righteous for the unrighteous, to bring you to God' (1 Pet. 3:18). So, with Paul, if we believe in Jesus we can say that 'the Son of God ... loved me and gave himself up for me' (Gal. 2:20).

It is, then, by the sacrificial death on Jesus on the cross that we have been 'redeemed'. That is, we have been rescued from the punishment for sin we deserve by the self-substitution of Jesus the Son of God on the cross for us. The price for our freedom from sin and death has been paid so that we are no longer our own, but we now belong to Jesus. He is the one who has 'redeemed us from all wickedness'. He has done so not only by dealing with the guilt of sin so that we can be forgiven, but also by dealing with the power of sin so that we can live for him and become godly. No longer are we enslaved to the 'wickedness' or literally the 'lawlessness' that once reigned in our hearts and controlled our lives. Because of his death for us Jesus has purified 'for himself a people that are his very own, eager to do what is good'. By the death of Jesus we have been cleansed of the guilt and shame and filth of sin.

And Jesus did this because he wants 'a people that are his very own'. That is, Jesus wants a people who are his treasured possession. The language here echoes that of Exodus 19:5 where God says that if Israel obeys him 'then out of all nations you will be my treasured possession'. As God's new covenant people we have been redeemed by Jesus to be his treasured possession and as such we are given grace to be 'eager to do what is good'. In the new covenant there is an eagerness to do the good that God commands (Jer. 31:33; Ezek. 36:26–27). From our hearts there is both the ability and the desire to live lives that are holy and godly. Where does such eagerness come from? It comes from the Holy Spirit who now indwells everyone who believes in Jesus. The Holy Spirit brings the grace that appeared in Jesus into our hearts so that we are eager to do what is good. To make that happen God's grace appeared in the person of Jesus Christ who gave himself for our redemption.

Do you know for yourself this grace that has appeared in Jesus? Have you turned to him from your sins and are you trusting in him as your Saviour? Don't assume you have simply because you have been christened or baptised, or raised in a Christian home or brought up to attend a Christian church. No, you must make this personal. You must personally repent of your sins and trust in Jesus Christ as offered to you in the gospel. It doesn't matter what kind of person you are since 'the grace of God has appeared [in Jesus] that offers salvation to all people'. Whoever you are, repent and believe in the Lord Jesus Christ and you will be saved. When you do you will know, as every Christian knows, that you have been redeemed by Jesus from all the wickedness in your life and that he has purified you to be a person who is 'his very own, eager to do what is good'. If you want to have your sins forgiven and to escape the tyranny of sin so that you can begin to change for good, then this is what must happen to you.

The grace of God now teaches us how to live

Having been saved by grace, grace now becomes our teacher of how to live as Christians:

> It teaches us to say 'No' to ungodliness and worldly passions, and to live self-controlled, upright and godly lives in this present age, while we wait for the blessed hope—the

appearing of the glory of our great God and Saviour, Jesus Christ (verses 12–13).

The word 'teaches' means not merely imparting information by instruction, but the whole-life training or discipline of a child. It is the same word translated as 'training' used by Paul in Ephesians 6:4 where he writes – 'Fathers, do not exasperate your children; instead bring them up in the training and instruction of the Lord'. What Paul is saying in verse 12 is that the grace that has appeared in Jesus Christ teaches us or trains us in a way similar to the way a father would teach or train his children. Think of a mother or father teaching a child how to ride a bike, to cook a meal or to learn a subject they love and want to pass on. Of course, this teaching necessarily involves imparting knowledge. As Christians we need to know and understand our faith if we are to live as Christians. But this teaching is also very practical in the way it enables us to learn how to live as Christians. It is important that if we are to live faithfully as Christians that we keep hold of both the doctrinal and practical aspects of what we are being taught. And if the Lord puts us in a position where we teach other Christians, we must make sure that what we teach is both doctrinal and practical.

In thinking about what it means for grace to teach us there are two questions to ask. First, what does grace teach us? There is a negative and a positive aspect to the answer to that question. Negatively, the grace of God teaches 'us to say "No" to ungodliness and worldly passions' (v. 12). We must renounce or repudiate 'ungodliness'. That is, we must reject decisively all that is contrary to God's will and opposed to him as revealed in his Word and thus is contrary to the devotion he wants from us. At the same time, we must renounce or repudiate 'worldly passions'. We must decisively reject the sinful desires or lusts for the world in its rebellion against God that come to shape and control us. In a word, we must say 'No' to sin in whatever form it takes. Really what Paul is writing about here is what he describes elsewhere as putting sin to death.

> Put to death, therefore, whatever belongs to your earthly nature: sexual immorality, impurity, lust, evil desires and greed, which is idolatry. Because of these, the wrath of God is coming. You used to walk in these ways, in the life you once lived. But now you must also rid yourselves of all such things as these: anger, rage, malice, slander, and filthy language from your lips (Col. 3:5–8).

This is what the old theologians called the mortification or the putting to death of sin. This is what we must be doing every day in relation to sin. Every day we must humble ourselves before God as we confess or acknowledge our sins before him and repent of them. Such repentance means rejecting our sins by turning from them to the Lord Jesus Christ for grace. In doing so, we will be forgiven. As the apostle John writes:

> If we claim to be without sin, we deceive ourselves and the truth is not in us. If we confess our sins, he is faithful and just and will forgive us our sins and purify us from all unrighteousness. (1 Jn. 1:8–9)

If genuine, such repentance will mean not only feeling bad about our sins, but it will also mean that, however imperfectly, we will begin to change our behaviour for good.

Which brings us to what grace teaches us positively. *Positively*, grace teaches us 'to live self-controlled, upright and godly lives in this present age'. Grace teaches us to live a 'self-controlled' life. Grace teaches us to control our appetites, desires and passions. Rather than being controlled by these things, *we* control *them*, enabling us to live in a way that pleases God. Like athletes in training for a competition, we discipline ourselves. Listen to how Paul describes his own self-control in 1 Corinthians 9:24–27,

> Do you not know that in a race all the runners run, but only one gets the prize? Run in such a way as to get the prize. Everyone who competes in the games goes into strict training. They do it to get a crown that will not last, but we do it to get a crown that will last forever. Therefore I do not run like someone running aimlessly; I do not fight like a boxer beating the air. No, I strike a blow to my body and make it my slave so that after I have preached to others, I myself will not be disqualified for the prize.

But grace also teaches us to live an 'upright' life. That is, grace teaches us to live in line with the righteousness of the moral law of God. There is no conflict between grace and law as some suppose. In the new covenant God's grace enables us to do what he commands. Augustine of Hippo famously prayed: 'Give me the grace to do as you command, and command me to do what you will!'[2] And as Augustine knew and every Christian knows from experience, God answers that prayer. Finally, grace teaches us to live a 'godly' life. As I have defined it, godliness is devotion to God actively expressed in a good life empowered by the gospel. A godly life is, then, a good life that in its various aspects is an active expression of our devotion to God. Such devotion embraces our worship and communion with God as well as our relationships, our work, our church life, our politics, our money, our education, our recreation and everything else.

If that is what grace teaches us, how does she do so? If you like, what is her method as a good teacher? Fundamentally, grace teaches us by changing our hearts. When we become Christians, when we are converted, we are given new birth so that we trust in Christ. United to Christ, we are no longer the people we once were, but we are now new creatures in him and as such now have the desire and ability to what is good, even though we still struggle with temptation and sin until we are glorified. And being Christians, God uses the Bible as we prayerfully read it, meditate upon it, and hear it read and preached in church. Indeed, God inspired the Bible and gives it to us because it 'is useful for teaching, rebuking, correcting and training in righteousness so that the servant of God may be thoroughly equipped for every good work' (2 Tim. 3:16–17). Other means of grace include baptism, the Lord's Supper and the fellowship of God's people. However, much as we need all this, we need something more: the Holy Spirit. Everyone who believes in Jesus has received the Holy Spirit and is indwelt by him. Among the many things the Spirit does in our lives as believers is to give us that eagerness and motivation to do what is good. He kindles in our hearts the thankfulness to Jesus for all he is and has done as our Saviour that motivates us to live for him.

However, the Spirit not only motivates, but he also *empowers* us to reject ungodly and worldly passions and to live self-controlled, upright and godly lives. We don't have the strength in ourselves to do that, but the Holy Spirit gives us the strength. On our part we may feel weak and powerless, but the Holy Spirit is present with us to make us strong and powerful. Indeed, his power is made perfect in our weakness so that with Paul we can say, 'For when I am weak, then I am strong' (2 Cor. 12:10). The Holy Spirit really is the secret of the Christian life. In our weakness the Holy Spirit is powerfully at work so that we say 'No' to all that is ungodly and 'Yes' to all that is godly.

All this happens 'in this present age, while we wait for the blessed hope – the appearing of the glory of our great God and Saviour, Jesus Christ' (v. 13). We live 'in this present age' when the saving reign of King Jesus has invaded a world in rebellion against him. Living as Christians in such a world we have a 'blessed hope'. We have a hope full of the promise of the blessing that will be ours when Jesus returns. The Lord Jesus Christ who first appeared in the humility of his birth will appear again in glory. And it will be the glory of Jesus as 'our great God and Saviour' that will appear. Paul, almost in passing, makes the astounding claim that the Jesus who is human is also God. He is the eternal Son of God who became a man. This Jesus, the God-man, will appear again in the human flesh he assumed in the womb of his virgin mother Mary but then it will be a glorified body because of his resurrection and ascension. But Jesus will also appear in the glory of his deity as the eternal Son of God. What a glorious sight that will be! But right now, 'in this present age', we wait for the appearing again of Jesus. That means living self-controlled, upright and godly lives. Living such lives in this world is not easy; it wasn't for Christians living on first-century Crete, and isn't for Christians living in twenty-first century Britain. But as we wait in hope, God gives us all the grace we need. He gives us the Holy Spirit who both motivates and empowers us to live to please him.

How amazing the grace of God is! From first to last, grace saves wretches like us who once were lost but now can see. Grace opens our hearts to believe and through all the dangers, toils and snares of life leads us home. And by his grace the Lord Jesus promises good to us and by his Word secures our hope so that 'when this mortal life is past and earthly days have ceased', we 'shall possess with Christ at last eternal joy and peace.' But right now, 'in this present age' as we wait for 'the appearing of the glory of our great God and Saviour, Jesus Christ' we can by God's amazing grace 'live self-controlled, upright and godly lives'. And as we do, each of us can say with John Newton that 'I am not what I ought to be, nor what I wish to be, nor what I hope to be ...[but] by the grace of God, I am what I am'. There's no sweeter sound to the sinner than the sound of God's amazing grace that has appeared in Jesus Christ.

Questions for discussion

1. What is the danger when a godly lifestyle is detached from the gospel of grace?

2. Why was godliness at the heart of the appearance of God's grace in Jesus Christ and how did his work of salvation make it possible?

3. Both negatively and positively, how does grace train us to be godly?

4. Why do we need to preach the gospel of grace to ourselves every day?

5. Why is the hope of the return of Jesus so important for nurturing a godly lifestyle?

Godly citizenship

Chapter 6

Godliness is expressed in the way Christians relate to the world as citizens (Titus 3:1–2)

The Christian life is a tale of two cities. Those two cities are not London and Paris as in the famous novel about the French Revolution by Charles Dickens. Rather, the Christian life is the tale of living as citizens of both the city of this world and the city of God. The city of this world is the community of people who live in the world at any time. The city of God is the community of all those who love God on earth and in heaven. And as Christians we are citizens of both cities. Our citizenship in the heavenly city of God is our primary citizenship. There we will live forever in the new creation and our first loyalty is to God and his city. But as Christians we are also citizens of the city of this world, where we live out our lives and do the ordinary things people do in the course of life. In the city of this world, we are to live the self-controlled, upright and godly lives that the gospel makes possible. For sure, such a godly lifestyle is about our personal devotion to God and how that is actively expressed in our relationships with people and not least as members of a local church. But a godly lifestyle is also about how our devotion to God is actively expressed as we live in this world.

In this chapter we are thinking about what it means to be godly citizens in this world. This is what Paul turns his attention to in chapter 3 of his letter to Titus. Having considered what it means to be godly in our personal relationships, he now turns his attention to what it means to be godly in the society around us. Godliness must go public as we live as citizens of the society in which God has placed us. And by 'citizens' I don't only mean that we are entitled to a passport in a particular country or that we can vote in elections. Being a citizen of the city of this world involves politics in the narrow sense of the word of voting and elections and so on, but it also involves how we relate to our neighbours, pay our taxes, obey the law, do our work, volunteer to help people, pray for government and generally seek the welfare of the society in which we live. Yes, we are citizens first of the eternal city of God and live as exiles from it in this world. But as the prophet Jeremiah told the Jewish exiles in Babylon, we are to live normal lives in this world as we 'seek the peace and prosperity of the city' in which God has put us and pray to him for it 'because if it prospers, [we] will prosper' (Jer. 29:7). So, in this chapter we are exploring what that means practically for us as the people of God not in sixth century BC

Babylon or in first century AD Crete but in twenty-first century Britain or wherever we are living.

And it is so important that we do this because the temptation for us as Christians is to privatise our faith. That's what the world would like us to do. The world is happy for us to believe what we want as long we keep it to ourselves and maybe to our families (although that is being challenged). What the world doesn't want is for our faith to go public and for us to live openly as followers of Jesus in what is sometimes called 'the public square'. Particularly in an increasingly aggressive secular culture like Britain that is the case. Except in its most anodyne form, religion and particularly Christian religion, is not acceptable in the media or politics or education and in public generally. So as Christians it is tempting to keep our heads down and to keep our Christianity private.

But we must resist this temptation. We must live out our Christianity – we must be godly – in the public square. Without shame we must live as Christian citizens in our society. We do this not because we want to take control of political or cultural power so that we can make the country a Christian theocracy, as some opponents of Christianity fear. No, we want to live openly as Christian citizens because we love our neighbours and therefore seek the welfare of our society and want people to flourish as human beings made in the image of God. Of course, how we live openly as Christians will be different for every Christian depending on our gifts, opportunities and circumstances. But what must be the same for all of us as Christians is that, however we do it, we live openly and unashamedly in the world as followers of Jesus. That's Paul's concern as he expresses it in 3:1–2,

> Remind the people to be subject to rulers and authorities, to be obedient, to be ready to do whatever is good, to slander no one, to be peaceable and considerate, and always to be gentle toward everyone.

Let's think about these words so that we know, first, *how* we should live and, second, *why* we should live as godly citizens in this world.

How we should live as godly citizens in this world

Paul begins by telling Titus to 'remind the people' (v. 1) about what it means to be citizens in the world. That he does this is significant. As Christians we need reminders because we can be very forgetful even about important things. In this case, like the Christians on Crete, we can forget that what is important is that our godliness is expressed in public as well as in private. For the simple reality is that life in this world is complicated and gets busy with many things so that we forget some things we need to remember. No doubt as believers got on with life on Crete in the first century, they wouldn't have given much thought to their citizenship in the wider world.

The same can be true of us. It's not that we want to live in a cocoon or cut ourselves off from unbelievers. The problem is that in getting on with life we forget to think about it as Christians. We can let ourselves go with the flow of our culture so that we live in the world pretty much like everyone else. We don't think biblically about how we live in the world. When that happens, we find ourselves conforming to the world so that it is hard to distinguish us from unbelievers. In the language of Jesus, we cease to be 'the salt of the earth' by losing our saltiness or what it is that makes us different as his disciples. What is it, then, that we, like the Cretan Christians, need to remember about being godly citizens in the world? There are seven things to note:

(1) A godly citizen is subject to rulers and authorities (v. 1)

As Christian citizens we are to 'be subject to rulers and authorities'. The 'rulers and authorities' are the state – that is, the governments, legal system, police and other institutions – that God has put in place as authorities in every society. Or perhaps I should say '*almost* every society', since there are some places where for various reasons there is anarchy. Few things are worse than when that happens and there is total disorder and chaos. Life for everyone, not only Christians, is very difficult. But generally speaking, there are in every society governing authorities of some kind, because that is what God has established in human society. For a fuller explanation of this we need to read what Paul writes in Romans 13:1–7,

> Let everyone be subject to the governing authorities, for there is no authority except that which God has established. The authorities that exist have been established by God. Consequently, whoever rebels against the authority is rebelling against what God has instituted, and those who do so will bring judgment on themselves. For rulers hold no

115

terror for those who do right, but for those who do wrong. Do you want to be free from fear of the one in authority? Then do what is right and you will be commended. For the one in authority is God's servant for your good. But if you do wrong, be afraid, for rulers do not bear the sword for no reason. They are God's servants, agents of wrath to bring punishment on the wrongdoer. Therefore, it is necessary to submit to the authorities, not only because of possible punishment but also as a matter of conscience. This is also why you pay taxes, for the authorities are God's servants, who give their full time to governing. Give to everyone what you owe them: If you owe taxes, pay taxes; if revenue, then revenue; if respect, then respect; if honour, then honour.

The 'rulers and authorities' Paul calls 'God's servant for your good' (Rom. 13:4). Paul doesn't have in mind here Christian rulers but pagan rulers. The infamous Nero was the Roman emperor when Paul wrote Romans and Titus, and it was probably under Nero's rule that he and others were martyred. Nevertheless, even a bad pagan ruler like Nero is God's servant for the good of people. Indeed, that is why we are to pay taxes and give them the respect and honour that is due them. Not only so, but we are to pray for those who govern us, as Paul writes in 1 Timothy 2:1–4,

I urge, then, first of all, that petitions, prayers, intercession and thanksgiving be made for all people—for kings and all those in authority, that we may live peaceful and quiet lives in all godliness and holiness. This is good, and pleases God our

Saviour, who wants all people to be saved and to come to a knowledge of the truth.

The optimal conditions for godly and holy Christian living, as well as for evangelism and missions, is a society in which everyone lives peacefully and quietly. That requires good government and therefore as Christians we must pray for our government. The apostle Peter says much the same as Paul in 1 Peter 2:13–14,

> Submit yourselves for the Lord's sake to every human authority: whether to the emperor, as the supreme authority, or to governors, who are sent by him to punish those who do wrong and to commend those who do right.

Of course, behind all that these apostles say are the well-known words of Jesus – 'Give to Caesar the things that are Caesar's, and to God the things that are God's' (Mk. 12:17). Christians are to give to rulers and authorities appropriate submission, but to give to God everything.

What does all this mean practically for us as Christians living in Britain today? To be subject to our government means that as Christians we accept its authority for the purposes God has established it. We are blessed to live in a democratic, constitutional monarchy with an elected parliament and an independent judiciary. We have the right to vote in elections for a government. We may or may not agree with everything that the elected government does, but we are to accept it as having been established by God. And the basic purpose for which God has established ours or any government is for it

117

to maintain law and order and to defend the country from internal and external enemies. For that reason, the government is given 'the sword' (Rom. 13:4) by God or sanctioned by him to administer justice and use physical force. In the United Kingdom as in most countries, government does many other things such as regulating the economy, providing education, running the health service, providing welfare and much else. And government is not only national but also at other levels such as, in the United Kingdom, the devolved administrations and local authorities. On whatever level, we subject ourselves to government by obeying the laws it makes and paying our taxes. That is what we are to do whatever form of government we live under. In the United Kingdom we live in a democracy, but many Christians live under authoritarian regimes of one kind or another. Some are very anti-Christian and persecute Christians. But whatever kind of government we live under, we are as Christians to subject ourselves to it as part of our obedience to Christ.

But there is a limit to our subjection to government. If what any government demands is contrary to the Word of God, we must then disobey it and suffer the consequences. When the apostles Peter and John were commanded by the religious authorities to stop preaching the gospel Peter said – 'We must obey God rather than human beings!' (Acts 5:25). No government has a right to prohibit the preaching of the gospel. Nor does any government have the right to compel Christians to participate in an abortion or to prevent parents from raising and disciplining their children in a way they believe is biblical, or to express what they think of transgenderism or same-sex marriage to name but a few examples. And there may be areas of life where Christians disagree but that in good conscience a Christian must do what he or she believes is right, such as not fighting in a war or refusing to conform to a religious requirement that other Christians do conform to. When our consciences, like that of Martin Luther at the Diet of Worms, are bound by the Word of God so that we can do nothing else, we must obey our consciences and not any human authority.

In doing so we accept the consequences, which may involve a penalty and even great suffering. But that is what is involved in following Jesus. And it seems to me that in years to come Christians will increasingly have to pay the cost of obeying God rather than human beings in a way that Christians in this country have not had to for a long time. But even then, as far as we can, we will as Christian citizens 'be subject to rulers and authorities'.

There is always the temptation for Christians to make submission to the governing authorities as an excuse to compromise when costly faithfulness is what is necessary. However, there are many examples from history of Christians submitting to the governing authorities but being compelled by their consciences to obey God rather than them. One example is the faithfulness of some 2000 Puritan ministers who in 1662 refused to accept the terms imposed on clergy in the Church of England with the result that they were ejected from their parishes at great cost to themselves and their families. In the subsequent decades Puritans, ministers and members, were

119

fiercely persecuted, the most famous perhaps being John Bunyan who was imprisoned for refusing to stop preaching. More recently, during the Second World War Protestant Christians in the small town of Chambon-sur-Lignon in France disobeyed the Vichy authorities by hiding thousands of Jews so that they would not be deported to concentration camps. In the Netherlands Christians such as the family of Corrie ten Boom did the same. In China during the Communist revolution the great preacher Wang Ming Dao refused to submit his preaching and ministry to the control of the Communist Party and with his wife was imprisoned for many years.[1] In the Soviet Union the Baptist pastor Georgi Vins and in Uganda Anglican Archbishop Janani Luwum did the same, the latter at the cost of his life, as have many under tyrannical regimes.

All these men and women believed that while as Christians they must 'be subject to rules and authorities' they nevertheless owed their primary obedience to God whatever the cost. In years to come we in Britain and the West may be called to suffer for being faithful to God. That is more likely to involve discrimination in some form rather than imprisonment, but when it comes we must be resolved as godly citizens to obey God even if it means disobeying human authorities.

(2) A godly citizen is obedient

It is not only governing authorities that Christians are to obey; they are to be 'obedient' (v. 1) to everyone. Here Paul seems to have in mind our obedience to other forms of authority in the world such as there are in where we work or study. Basically, as

Christians we should obey the rules. Paul has made this point in what he has said to slaves in 2:9–10,

> Teach slaves to be subject to their masters in everything, to try to please them, not to talk back to them, and not to steal from them, but to show that they can be fully trusted, so that in every way they will make the teaching about God our Saviour attractive.

Paul is even more explicit in Ephesians 6:5–8,

> Slaves, obey your earthly masters with respect and fear, and with sincerity of heart, just as you would obey Christ. Obey them not only to win their favour when their eye is on you, but as slaves of Christ, doing the will of God from your heart. Serve wholeheartedly, as if you were serving the Lord, not people, because you know that the Lord will reward each one for whatever good they do, whether they are slave or free.

I dealt with the issue of slavery in chapter 4 and readers may want to refer to that again. Here my point is simply that what Paul wrote to slaves can be applied in principle to everyone who works under someone else. We should do the work we are employed to do and in the way we are contracted to do it. Of course, unlike slaves we have rights at work and there are usually ways to make grievances known, often through a trade union. And as with our subjection to government, so with our obedience at work, there are limits. No one at work has a right to command us to do something that is sinful such as lying or stealing. But even then, we should not be insubordinate and make things difficult in the workplace. That applies as well to school and university. We should abide by the rules even when we can work to change them for the better.

(3) A godly citizen is ready to do whatever is good

Our general rule in relating to the world is to 'be ready to do whatever is good' (v.1) wherever we are. As Paul writes in Galatians 6:10, 'Therefore, as we have opportunity, let us do good to all people, especially to those who belong to the family of believers'. In his first letter Peter says much the same:

> Dear friends, I urge you, as foreigners and exiles, to abstain from sinful desires, which wage war against your soul. Live such good lives among the pagans that, though they accuse you of doing wrong, they may see your good deeds and glorify God on the day he visits us. (1 Pet. 2:11–12)

Even when non-Christians treat us badly, indeed especially then, we are to do them good:

> Do not repay evil with evil or insult with insult. On the contrary, repay evil with blessing, because to this you were called so that you may inherit a blessing. For,
>
> "Whoever would love life
> and see good days
> must keep their tongue from evil
> and their lips from deceitful speech.
> They must turn from evil and do good;
> they must seek peace and pursue it.

For the eyes of the Lord are on the righteous
    and his ears are attentive to their prayer,
but the face of the Lord is against those who do evil."

Who is going to harm you if you are eager to do good? (1 Pet. 3:9–13a)

Even if it costs us, Christians should be benefactors in the world. With the package of gifts, opportunities and circumstances God gives each of us at various stages in life we should be doing good in all kinds of ways. That might mean simply being a good neighbour by helping someone or volunteering in some way that benefits people and helps them to flourish as human beings. Some Christians may believe that loving their neighbours and doing good means getting involved in politics at some level for the good of the city or nation. Still others will be involved in education, the media, work, sports, the arts and the wider culture. There are many things we can do as citizens both through the church and outside it in the world.

As Christians we have a great heritage of people who have made the world a better place by doing good. In the fast-changing society of nineteenth century Britain, with its expanding industries and growing cities, there were many social problems that evangelical Christians sought to remedy. Some, like Lord Shaftesbury, did much in Parliament to improve working conditions in factories and mines among other things. Elizabeth Fry both visited prisoners and led Bible studies in prisons, but she also campaigned for prison reform. Others such as the Congregationalist minister Andrew Reed in east London and the Brethren leader George Muller in Bristol set up orphanages. As well as his orphanages, Thomas Barnardo set up 'ragged schools' for poor children as did many Christians and churches. Nonconformist industrialists such as Sir Titus Salt in Bradford and Samuel Morley in Nottingham and London sought to improve the living and working conditions of their employees, as well as in Morley's case to become a Member of Parliament.

One of the most remarkable examples of doing good in this period was Ellen Ranyard who founded the London Bible and Domestic Mission in 1857. Mrs Ranyard was the wife of a Nonconformist businessman who was touched by the plight of the young women selling flowers and other things in the Covent Garden area of London. As well as herself she began to organise other women to visit them with Bibles and evangelistic tracts but was soon also organising medical and other forms of practical support for poor women all over the city. The Ranyard Bible Mission, as it was popularly known, became one of the largest domestic missions in the country. Today the midwifery, district nursing and social work professions acknowledge their origins in the good Ellen Ranyard did. If there is good to do, we as Christians must be ready to do it with the gifts, circumstances and opportunities that the Lord has given each of us. Such doing of good makes the world a better place and is what we should be known for as Christians in the world.

(4) A godly citizen slanders no one

How quick people are to 'slander' (v. 2) other people especially when in a controversy of some kind. To slander someone means to speak evil of them. We're not to think the worst of people and say so to other people. Of course, we're not naive and on occasion may need to talk about someone's bad character or behaviour. But our intention must not be to malign someone in order to maliciously destroy their reputation. Sadly, that is what all too many are all ready to do. Once, slander was something that happened mostly in private conversation or correspondence and in tabloid newspapers, but today social media gives vastly more opportunity for this. On X (formerly Twitter) or a similar platform someone's reputation can be trashed within minutes all over the planet. People post the most horrible things about other people, who re-post it to others and on it goes. As Christian citizens we must have no part in this. We must watch what we think about people and then what we say about them.

(5) A godly citizen is peaceable

Being 'peaceable' (v. 2) as Christians means that we should not be contentious and argumentative, always stirring up strife between people. There is so much of that in the world. It is said of some people that if you left them alone in a room, they would get in a fight with themselves. When strife happens on a large scale it can be very destructive to families, communities and nations. Rather than get caught up in such strife we should be peacemakers who seek to reconcile people. Of course, we don't seek peace at all costs and sometimes peace cannot be made. But as far as we should, we seek to be channels of God's peace in this world (Mt. 5:9, 38–48; Rom. 12:17–21).

(6) A godly citizen is considerate

The idea of being 'considerate' (v. 2) is of a gentleness that is seen in the graciousness and consideration we should have for other people. Rather than being brash and pushy with people, we should gently consider their situation and seek to help them. We should be kind to people in the way we treat them. It is the opposite of treating someone severely. In some ways we could say that a Christian citizen is a true gentleman or gentlewoman in the way he or she treats people. Couldn't the world do with more such people in the public square whether in political office or simply as neighbours? Christians should be models of civility.

(7) A godly citizen is always gentle towards everyone

The idea of being 'gentle towards everyone' (v. 2) is similar to the peaceableness we just thought about. As Christians we are to be courteous as we reflect the gentleness and meekness of Jesus in our relationships with non-Christians as well as with Christians. One commentator says it is the opposite of 'roughness, bad temper, sudden anger and brusqueness' (G. McKnight).[2] In some cultures, such behaviour is almost a virtue, but as followers of a meek and gentle Saviour that mustn't be true of us. That doesn't mean we should be timid and unassertive pushovers. Jesus certainly wasn't, but like him we can express our courage and strength through the gentleness with which we deal with even the most difficult people.

Here, then, is a profile of a godly citizen. Is this the kind of citizen you are? Are you subject to the rulers and authorities in this country or wherever you live? Are you obedient to the other authorities under which you live? Are you ready to do whatever is good with your particular gifts, opportunities and circumstances? Are you slandering no one, but rather speaking well of people? Are you peaceable when others are contentious? Are you considerate in the way you treat people? Are you always gentle towards everyone as Jesus was?

Godly citizens like that can make a big difference for good in the world. Godly citizens like that really are the salt and light of the world. They may not be well known and may achieve little that people notice. But quietly they affect the lives of other people and their communities for good. In ways we cannot plan or imagine God uses such godly citizens to change the world for good. Of course, that's not all we do. As Christians we also do all we can to see that the gospel is preached so the people will be saved. Such gospel preaching is, with prayer, the priority of the church. But even if people do not respond positively to the preaching of the gospel, we can still do them good as we live faithfully and openly as godly Christian citizens in this world.

But how is that possible?

Why we can live as godly citizens in the world

The reason we can live as godly Christian citizens in the world is simply because we have been saved by God. That's the reason Paul gives in verses 3–7:

> At one time we too were foolish, disobedient, deceived and enslaved by all kinds of passions and pleasures. We lived in malice and envy, being hated and hating one another. But when the kindness and love of God our Saviour appeared, he saved us, not because of righteous things we had done, but because of his mercy. He saved us through the washing of rebirth and renewal by the Holy Spirit, whom he poured out on us generously through Jesus Christ our Saviour, so that, having been justified by his grace, we might become heirs having the hope of eternal life.

What a glorious statement of the gospel! We will dig more into these verses in the next chapter. At this point, suffice it to say that the reason we can live as godly citizens is because a great change has happened to us. That is what had happened to the Christians on Crete with the result that they no longer lived and behaved as they once did. Like them each of us who is a Christian has experienced the great change that is conversion. In his kindness, love and mercy God has saved us not because of anything we have done, but because of what he has done in the Lord Jesus Christ. And having trusted in God for salvation we no longer live for ourselves or what this world esteems, but to do what is good.

This life-transforming gospel, that benefits not only Christians but everyone, must be preached and taught as Paul exhorted Titus in verse 8,

> This is a trustworthy saying. And I want you to stress these things, so that those who have trusted in God may be careful to devote themselves to doing what is good. These things are excellent and profitable for everyone.

The evidence that the gospel changes people to do good is seen in history and around the world today. Of course, Christians have not always been the good citizens they should be. None of us has. And some Christians have done or tolerated bad things in the name of Christ. But on the whole, gospel Christianity has done the world much good. In East London where I was a pastor for thirty-five years, much good was done by people like Andrew Reed, Elizabeth Fry, Thomas Barnardo, Archibald Brown and William and Catherine Booth to name a few. But let me call as a witness an atheist. Matthew Parris was a Member of Parliament who now writes for *The Times*. A few years ago, he wrote this after a trip to his native Africa:

> Now a confirmed atheist, I've become convinced of the enormous contribution that Christian evangelism makes in Africa: sharply distinct from the work of secular NGOs, government projects and international aid efforts. These alone will not do. Education and training alone will not do. In Africa Christianity changes people's hearts. It brings a spiritual transformation. The rebirth is real. The change is good.[3]

That is what the gospel does in Africa or Europe or anywhere in the world. By the gospel we are saved from the wrath to come and have the hope of eternal life with the result that we are changed to do good. That change is seen not only in our personal lives and relationships, but also in how to live in this world as godly citizens. Living in this world as Christians is indeed a tale of two cities. Let's make sure, then, that as citizens of the heavenly city of God we live faithfully as citizens of the city of this world, doing as much good as we can.

Questions for discussion

1. Why is it important that we think of godliness in relation not only to ourselves and our churches, but also in the way we relate to non-Christians and to the world?

2. What does it mean for us as Christians to live in this world as citizens of heaven, much like the Jewish exiles in Babylon?

3. What do the seven characteristics of godly citizens mean for us practically in whatever country we are living in? Take time to discuss each one.

4. How does politics as it is often conducted in the world contrast with what Paul writes here about how Christians are to engage in politics?

5. What is the best way for Christians to see change for good in any society?

Chapter 7

It is the gospel of grace that enables us to be godly citizens (Titus 3:3-8)

This world should be a better place because there are Christians. This world is certainly a better place because William Wilberforce was a Christian[1]. He is famously the man who headed the political campaign in Parliament that led to the abolition of the slave trade in the British Empire in 1807 and eventually to the abolition of slavery in 1833. Many others inside and outside of Parliament were also involved in the campaign to abolish slavery, but Wilberforce was at its heart.

And he was because he was a Christian. He was converted in 1785 in part through reading a book entitled *The Rise and Progress of Religion in the Soul* by the Congregationalist minister Philip Doddridge. That book made Wilberforce realise that genuine Christianity was more than merely a system of religion to which people must conform but was also a living relationship with God through faith in Jesus Christ who saves people and changes their lives from the inside out. Later Wilberforce also wrote a book with the shortened title of *A Practical View* in which he described this 'real Christianity' in contrast to what many people in his day thought Christianity was.[2]

Not long after his conversion, Wilberforce thought about becoming an Anglican minister, but on the advice of John Newton he decided to remain a politician so that he could not only campaign for the abolition of slavery, but also work to see the condition of society improved in other ways. In his generation there were many others like Wilberforce such as his fellow abolitionist Oloudah Equiano, the prison reformer John Howard and the writer Hannah More, who all made the world a better place because of their real Christianity.

That should also be the case in our world today, because there are Christians making a difference *because* they are Christians. To make the world a better place doesn't mean that we have to be politicians like Wilberforce, although that is what God may call some of us to be. But each of us has been called by God to serve him by doing good during our lives in this world. So that we can do good, God has given each of us a unique package of gifts, opportunities and circumstances. We are unlikely to be remembered in history like Wilberforce. But in our little ways we can make this world a better place because we are Christians. The seemingly little things we do, such as being a parent governor in a school, helping in a night shelter for the homeless, or mentoring a troubled child, can be used by God to accomplish far greater things than we could ever have imagined. God weaves the little things every Christian does into the tapestry of the bigger things he is doing in the world. Whatever our gifts, circumstances and opportunities, as Christians we can do good and make this world a better place.

In Titus 3:3–8 we discover why it is that as Christians we can do good so that the world is a better place. As he writes to Titus, the apostle Paul has turned to the subject of how Christians should relate to the world. Having described in verses 1–2 the kind of godly citizens we should be as Christians, Paul goes on in verses 3–8 to explain why we can be such citizens. The reason is that God has saved us. Here is how Paul describes his salvation in verses 3–7:

> At one time we too were foolish, disobedient, deceived and enslaved by all kinds of passions and pleasures. We lived in malice and envy, being hated and hating one another. But when the kindness and love of God our Saviour appeared, he saved us, not because of righteous things we had done, but because of his mercy. He saved us through the washing of rebirth and renewal by the Holy Spirit, whom he poured out on us generously through Jesus Christ our Saviour, so that, having been justified by his grace, we might become heirs having the hope of eternal life.

God has 'saved us' (v. 5). What have we been saved from? We have been saved from God's 'coming wrath' as Paul puts it elsewhere (1 Thes. 1:9) or from perishing forever as we're told in John 3:16. And God has saved us not because we deserve it. On the contrary, it wasn't 'because of the righteous things we had done'. God hasn't saved us because we were really good at religion and morality. At their best 'our righteous acts are but like filthy rags' as the prophet Isaiah describes them (Isa. 64:6). No, we have been saved because of God's mercy on us as sinners. God saw us in our desperate plight and did something to save us in Jesus Christ. We want to think about what it means to be saved by God in his mercy and how that should motivate us to do good so that this world is a better place.

There are two key things to note from the passage.

Saved by God, we are not the people we were before becoming Christians

Paul begins by reminding the Cretan Christians what they once were like before their conversions: 'At one time we too were foolish, disobedient, deceived and enslaved by all kinds of passions and pleasures. We lived in malice and envy, being hated and hating one another'. It's not a pretty picture of life before Christ. Note the word 'we'. Paul is identifying himself with the Cretans. What was true of the Cretans was just as true of him, who as a devout Jew had been very religious and sought to obey God's law. What Paul writes here about the Cretans and himself applies in principle to every Christian whatever their lifestyle before becoming Christians. It doesn't matter if we had been moral reprobates who broke all the rules or morally upright churchgoers who never did a thing wrong, or someone in between the two. Whatever form it took we needed to be saved from our sinful rebellion against God. We must never forget who we once were before we became a Christian.

Let's look more closely at what we once were. There are three things to note.

(1) We were once foolish and disobedient

Our thinking was 'foolish' not in that we were stupid and unintelligent, but that we did not have a real understanding of God and his salvation. It is what Paul means in Romans 1:21 where he writes that 'their thinking became futile and their foolish hearts were darkened' and in Ephesians 4:18 where he writes about unbelievers:

> They are darkened in their understanding and separated from the life of God because of the ignorance that is in them due to the hardening of their hearts.

Once we were like that in the way we foolishly rejected the gospel. And in our foolishness we were also 'disobedient'. That is, we disobeyed what God commands us to do or forbids not to do in his law. If we had some knowledge of the Bible we would have known very clearly what God has commanded, but nevertheless defiantly disobeyed him. But even if we had no knowledge of the Bible, the moral law of God was written in our consciences (Rom. 2:14–15). We disobeyed God in spite of knowing right and wrong in the most basic way. For that reason, we were under the judgment of God and faced his eternal wrath because of our sins.

(2) We were once deceived and enslaved by all kinds of passions and pleasures

We like to think that we are clear-sighted about life and know what is what. But the reality was that we were 'deceived'. We were deceived by *the world* that would have us believe that what it thinks is important – power, image, money, control and so on – is what matters. We were deceived by *ourselves* so that although we knew the truth about God and what he demands we suppressed it in our wickedness (Rom. 1:18–20). And we were deceived by *the devil* who unknown to us blinded us in unbelief as he held us captive in the fear of death.

However, it wasn't only that we were deceived, but also that we were 'enslaved to all kinds of passions and pleasures'. How we like to think that as human beings we are free to live as we want and do as we choose. But the reality is that we are slaves. We are slaves to our 'passions'. Our passions or desires, which are not necessarily bad in themselves, are the things that control us, and not our minds as we like to think. The things that we want most in life – career, family, financial security or whatever – become the false gods we slavishly serve rather than the true God to whom service is true freedom. When twisted by sin such passions become tyrants that can destroy us and those we love. But it is also 'pleasures' that enslave us. The things in life that God has given us to enjoy – food and drink and friends and so much more – can become our slave masters when we live for them rather than for God. They become toxic and poison our lives even as we enjoy them, like a spiked cocktail. Isn't such slavery to passions and pleasures what characterises life in our world today? But as Paul tells us in 2 Timothy 3:4 we must expect that in this time between the first and second comings of Jesus people will be 'lovers of pleasure rather than lovers of God'. How true that is.

(3) We once lived in malice and envy, being hated and hating one another

What once characterised our relationships with people was 'malice and envy'. John Stott calls these 'very ugly twins'.[3] Maliciously we have thought and may have spoken evil of people. We wished evil would happen to people we disliked or envied. Someone had something we wanted and in our envy we would maliciously think or say something about them. Even if our envy never expressed itself it could rage in our hearts and eat us up from the inside. All that is really just a form of hatred.

Sadly, 'being hated and hating one another' is all too common in human relationships. Such hatred expresses itself in many ways. It can be seen in the breakdown of a marriage or in a dispute at work or in political disagreements. But perhaps in our times and culture this is nowhere more evident than on the internet when Twitter mobs attack someone for saying something deemed unacceptable. It is quite astounding the hateful abuse some people receive from people who claim to be fighting a good and just cause.

Here, then, is a picture of what we once were. And what an ugly picture it is. It may or may not be exactly a picture of you before you became a Christian. If it isn't, thank God for his restraining mercy for if the circumstances of your life had been different, it could have been you. Any of us are capable of the worst human depravity. But this picture may be a very exact picture of your life before becoming a Christian. If that is the case, thank God that in his mercy he has saved you from this life. But however exact the picture is of you individually, remember that in principle this is what you once were and are no longer because of God's mercy and remember that this is what unbelievers still are and will remain unless God has mercy and saves them too.

What we read here should motivate us to evangelism and missions. We want to see people such as Paul describes saved as they hear the gospel and respond by repenting of their sins and trusting in Jesus as their Saviour and Lord. If you are not a Christian, then that is what you need to do right now. But as well as preaching the gospel individually and together as a church we also want to do good to people in this world whether or not they are Christians. We do so not because we now think we are better than non-Christians. How could we since we once were in the same condition as they are? That we are not now is not because of anything we did but because God had mercy on us. As the recipients of mercy, we want then to be merciful to others. But to do that we need to appreciate the depths of God's saving mercy to us as sinners.

Saved by God we are now the people we are after becoming Christians

In verses 4–7 we have one of the richest summaries of the gospel of our salvation in the Bible. It is amazing that in this short letter there are two such summaries, the other being in 2:11–14. In verses 4–7 Paul tells us two staggering things about what God has done in saving sinners like us. First, Paul tells us that in saving us, God has done something for us in Jesus Christ. Second, Paul tells us that in saving us, God has done something in us by the Holy Spirit. If we are to understand our salvation, we need to understand these two aspects of it. Put another way, our salvation as Christians is the work of our Triune Saviour God. The Father sent his Son to accomplish our salvation who then gives us the Holy Spirit so that he applies it to us. The Father, the Son and the Holy Spirit work as one for our salvation. Let's think about this more as we dig into these verses so that we understand the people that we now are as Christians saved by God.

(1) We are now the people we are because of what Jesus Christ has done for us

How can we describe what God has done in Jesus to save sinners like us? It can hardly be better described than as it is in verse 4 – 'But when the kindness and love of God our Saviour appeared'. We were in the terrible plight we have just been considering, but in his kindness and love God intervened to saved us. What a glorious 'But' that is in verse 4! It was because of his kindness and love that our Saviour God planned and carried out our salvation.

The idea of 'kindness' is that of goodness and generosity. It is goodness actively expressed in what someone does for the benefit of someone else. We all know people who have been kind to us, but how much more is kindness characteristic of God. The Greek word here for 'love' is the one we get our English word 'philanthropy' from. The idea is that of love for people being expressed in doing them good in some practical way.

In the past as well as the present, our country has benefited greatly from the philanthropy of people who used their resources to do good to other people in some way. At its best such philanthropy is a pale echo of the goodness and love of God. And the good God has done in his kindness and love as our Saviour was to send his Son. It is in Jesus Christ that 'the kindness and love of God our Saviour has appeared' in human flesh. The birth, the life, the death and the resurrection of Jesus reveal the kindness and love of our Saviour God. In that way we have been saved from the coming wrath. That wasn't because we deserved it in some way. On the contrary, we have not been saved 'because of righteous things we have done'. No, it was 'because of [God's] mercy' to undeserving sinners. As Charles Wesley has us sing, 'Tis mercy all, immense and free'.

And where this mercy, this love and kindness of God, is supremely seen is on the cross where Jesus died. On the cross Jesus atoned for the sins of his people by substituting himself in our place and suffering the penalty of death we deserved. He 'suffered once for all, the righteous for the unrighteous, to bring [us] to God' (1 Pet. 3:18). On the basis of the sacrificial death of Jesus we are 'justified by his grace' (v. 7). Graciously God declares us righteous and forgives our sins.

He does so because 'we have trusted in God' (v. 8). It is through faith in Jesus Christ that we are justified. God credits us with the righteousness of his Son so that not only are we forgiven, but we are accepted by him and then adopted into his family. That's why we have 'become heirs having the hope of eternal life' (v. 7). Justified through faith in Christ and adopted as his sons we are now 'heirs of God and co-heirs with Christ' (Rom. 8:17). In saving us God has given us an eternal inheritance in the new creation. As Paul puts it in 1 Corinthians 2:9,

> "What no eye has seen,
>> what no ear has heard,
> and what no human mind has conceived"—
>> the things God has prepared for those who love him"...

The God who does not lie has promised us eternal life. That is our hope as those whom God our Saviour in his kindness and love has justified through faith in Jesus Christ. This is what in saving us God has done for us in Jesus Christ. That is in part why we are now the people we are. No longer the people we were, we are now the people we are because 'the kindness and love of God our Saviour appeared' for our salvation in Jesus Christ. The question each one of us must answer is this: am I now someone whom God in his kindness and love has saved through the finished work of Jesus Christ? How do you answer?

(2) We are now the people we are because of what the Holy Spirit has done in us

Salvation is not only what God has done for us in Jesus Christ, but also what God has done in us by the Holy Spirit. As Paul writes in verse 5,

> He saved us through the washing of rebirth and renewal by the
> Holy Spirit, whom he poured out on us generously through
> Jesus Christ our Saviour, so that, having been justified by his
> grace, we might become heirs having the hope of eternal life.

What is this 'washing of rebirth and renewal by the Holy Spirit'? Is Paul talking about two things or one thing? I think he is talking about one thing with two aspects. The one thing is the work of the Holy Spirit in the life of a Christian. There would be no Christian life without the work of the Spirit. If it wasn't for the Holy Spirit nothing that Jesus accomplished for us would make any difference to our lives. It is the Holy Spirit who comes to indwell us and unite us to Jesus so that we can enjoy the blessings of all he accomplished for our salvation into our lives. This is why the Father has poured out the Holy Spirit through his risen and exalted Son. As Paul writes in verse 6 – 'whom he poured on us generously through Jesus Christ our Saviour', echoing what the apostle Peter said on the Day of Pentecost – 'Exalted to the right hand of God, he has received from the Father the promised Holy Spirit and has poured out what you now see and hear' (Acts 2:33). Ever since, the Holy Spirit is received by everyone who believes in Jesus as he is poured into their hearts. As Paul puts it in Romans 5:5, 'God's love has been poured out into our hearts through the Holy Spirit, who has been given to us'. And how generous God is in giving us the Holy Spirit! There is no stinting with the Spirit; he is 'poured out on us generously'. He is lavished on us. Being a Christian is unthinkable without the Holy Spirit.

The first aspect of the work of the Holy Spirit in us is that it begins with the 'rebirth'. The word translated 'rebirth' can also be translated 'regeneration'. The idea is that life is given where there was none before, as when a new life is conceived in the womb of a mother, or a dead person is raised to life. This is what Jesus spoke about to Nicodemus in terms of being born again (Jn. 3:3,5), and what Paul means in Ephesians 2:3–4 where he says that 'God ... made us alive with Christ'. When this happens there is a 'washing' away of sins as we trust in Jesus to save us. The outward sign of this washing is baptism, but the inward reality is that through faith we are cleansed of the guilt and stain of sins. The 'washing of rebirth' is where everything begins in the Christian life, when through the Word God gives rebirth or new birth to us. Like a seed with physical life in it, God plants new spiritual life in our souls. But that new spiritual life continues to grow and never will die.

The second aspect of the Holy Spirit's work is that with the 'washing of rebirth' the Holy Spirit also brings about 'renewal'. This renewal may be the same thing as the 'rebirth', but it also seems to suggest not so much the Holy Spirit's work at the beginning of the Christian life as his ongoing work in the life of a Christian. The Greek word can also be translated 'renovation'. And that is what the Holy Spirit is doing in a Christian's life. Imagine a great house that has fallen into disrepair and dilapidation. It's a wreck. But someone buys the house and as the owner moves in, he immediately reconnects the electricity, gas and water. He lights fires in the hearths. Then slowly he begins to renovate the house so that it will be restored to its original grandeur.

That's what the Holy Spirit is doing in each of our lives if we are Christians. Because of sin, the image of God in us has not been lost but it has been severely damaged. But when we become Christians, the Holy Spirit reconnects us with the life of God and then begins the process of renovation that will only be completed when we die and when we see Jesus at his return in power and glory. Then we will be perfectly conformed to the image of the Son of God. Until then we live by faith as the Holy Spirit works with us so that we are transformed by his sanctifying grace.

All this is involved in us as Christians becoming 'heirs having the hope of eternal life'. In the gospel the God who does not lie (1:1) has promised eternal life to all who believe in Jesus Christ. The very character of God guarantees the eternal salvation of every believer. That means that having been justified through faith and indwelt by the Spirit we are now the heirs of what God has promised.

In this world the children of rich people are often promised an inheritance in the future. As children of God, we are promised an infinitely greater inheritance in the new creation – eternal life in all its fullness. This inheritance that, as the apostle Peter puts it, 'can never perish, spoil or fade' unlike the wealth of this world, is right now being kept in heaven for us until it is fully revealed at the return of Jesus (1 Pet. 1:3–5). That is our hope as Christians, and in this life we live as heirs in the hope of inheriting all that God has promised. What an amazing thing it is to be a Christian!

Do you understand, then, why we are no longer the people we were, but are now the people we are? It is because of what Jesus Christ did *for us* in his life, death and resurrection and it is because of what the Holy Spirit did *in us* and continues to do in us by his washing of rebirth and renewal. Salvation is about both what God has done for us and what God has done – and continues to do – in us. And salvation is also about the hope of what God will do when Jesus returns. Practically what this means is that we have the motivation and the power to do what is good. As Paul writes in verse 8,

> This is a trustworthy saying. And I want you to stress these things, so that those who have trusted in God may be careful to devote themselves to doing what is good. These things are excellent and profitable for everyone.

God has been so good to us by having mercy on us as sinners in sending his Son to save us and then giving us the Holy Spirit. Because of what our Saviour God has done for us and in us to save us, we must devote ourselves to doing what is good. To underline his point Paul makes it one last time in verse 14: 'Our people must learn to devote themselves to doing what is good, in order to provide for urgent needs and not live unproductive lives'. Saved by God, not because of righteous things we have done but because of his mercy, we must eagerly devote ourselves to doing good. That's why William Wilberforce and many like him did so much good and made the world a better place.

I began this chapter by mentioning William Wilberforce but let me end by mentioning someone very different, in a different place and different time. His name is Tiyo Soga. He belonged to the Xhosa people in what is today South Africa. Born in 1829, he became a minister in the Presbyterian churches in South Africa in 1856, having trained for the ministry in Scotland. Later, his sons also studied in Scotland, one of whom became the first indigenous doctor in South Africa. In 2011 his stature was publicly recognised when a bust was unveiled in his home village by the then President of South Africa, Thabo Mbeki. After Tiyo Soga's death in 1871 a tablet was placed in a church that reads:

> He was a friend of God, a lover of his Son, inspired by his Spirit, a disciple of His holy Word. A zealous churchman, an ardent patriot, a large-hearted philanthropist, a dutiful son, an affectionate brother, a tender husband, a loving father, a faithful friend, a learned scholar, an eloquent orator and in manners a gentleman. A model [African] for the imitation and inspiration of his countrymen.[4]

Countless other examples could be chosen. The point is that that is what the gospel does. By the gospel we are saved from the wrath to come and have the hope of eternal life with the result that we are changed to do good. That change is seen not only in our personal lives and relationships, but also in how we live in this world as godly citizens. Living in this world as

Christians is indeed a tale of two cities. Let's make sure, then, that as citizens of the heavenly city of God we also live faithfully in this world as citizens of the city of this world, doing as much good as we can.

Questions for discussion

1. Why does Paul contrast our pre-conversion and post-conversion lives?

2. If you were religious and morally upright before your conversion, why does what Paul writes still apply to you? You may want to look at Ps. 51:3–5; Jer. 17:9; Mk. 7:20–23; Rom. 3:9–20; Eph. 2:1–10; 1 Tim. 1:15–16.

3. Why does what God has done for us in Christ make us better citizens?

4. Why does what God has done in us by the Holy Spirit make us better citizens?

5. You may not be William Wilberforce or Tiyo Soga, but how can you do good as a Christian citizen wherever you are because of the gospel of grace?

Conclusion

Chapter 8

Godliness is established by the advance of the gospel in the world (Titus 3:8-15)

It is the responsibility of every generation of Christians to advance the gospel where they are. We are to do all we can in the time and place where God has put us to see that the gospel makes headway in the world. We can't be complacent and take it for granted that that will happen. For the simple truth is that if we are not faithful in advancing the gospel it will retreat and may not even survive where we are. That may take time to happen, but in time it will. Sadly, that is what has happened in many churches and denominations in this country and around the world. Once flourishing churches are no more. Denominations and movements that once stood for the gospel and did much in the advance of the kingdom of Christ now tolerate and preach another gospel. Of course, there are other reasons why even faithful churches and denominations decline and die. For example, if the neighbourhood of a church changes so that there are fewer Christians and more people of another religion living in it, that church may find it hard to survive no matter how faithful it is. And it also needs to be said that even the most faithful and spiritually alive churches can go through periods of decline. But generally speaking, churches survive and thrive because faithful Christians advance the gospel where they are in their generation. And while that may involve a lot of hard work and a struggle and there may be great hostility, it can be done.

Living as we do in a culture that is increasingly hostile to biblical Christianity it is imperative that we understand what advancing the gospel involves. But the Cretan Christians had to advance the gospel in the hostile environment of their culture and therefore what Paul wrote to Titus and to them has much to teach us about advancing the gospel in the hostile environment of our culture.

But how are we to do that? What we're not to do is to use worldly means and methods to advance the gospel. That's always the temptation for the church. With even the best of intentions the church can seek political power and influence or emulate worldly models of leadership and organisation. They can imbibe unbiblical philosophies in the study of the Bible and theology, or uncritically adopt approaches to public worship that owe more to the world than the Word. No, if we want to see the gospel advance in the world then we must do what we can in line with what the Bible teaches. What Paul writes in these final verses of his letter to Titus can help us. He highlights several things that Titus and the Cretan Christians need to do to advance the gospel in the towns of the island of Crete. Some of the things Paul says are very clear and to the point, while others are more indirect and inferred from what he writes. I suggest that what the Cretan Christians needed to know in the first-century we need to know in the twenty-first century. What Paul writes gives us a framework for advancing the gospel where we are as Christians today. For each of us that practically means advancing the gospel through our particular local church, whether we are leaders or members. For as long as the Lord puts us in a church it is our responsibility to build on what others have done in advancing the gospel in our generation.

There are seven things we need to do to advance the gospel so that godliness is established.

1. Keep the gospel at the heart of the church by making sure it is preached

If the gospel is to be advanced in and by any church, it must be known and kept at its heart. That's why Paul tells Titus that what he has just written in verses 3–7 is trustworthy:

> This is a trustworthy saying. And I want you to stress these things, so that those who have trusted in God may be careful to devote themselves to doing what is good. These things are excellent and profitable for everyone (v. 8).

In 1 and 2 Timothy and here in Titus, Paul underlines words or sayings he wants to emphasise by referring to them as trustworthy sayings. These are bold statements that we can trust and rely on. In this case, what Paul wants to emphasise is the gospel he has just summarised in verses 3–7, just as he did earlier in 2:11–14. The gospel is about what God has done to save people like us from sin and its consequences by the Lord Jesus Christ. And God 'has saved us, not because of righteous things we had done, but because of his mercy' (v. 5). By both what Jesus did in his life, death and resurrection and what the Holy Spirit does in applying that to us, we are saved by God.

And not only are we saved from God's coming wrath and have 'the hope of eternal life', but having been given rebirth and renewal 'by the Holy Spirit, whom [God] poured out generously through Jesus Christ our Saviour' we are changed now as the result of his sanctifying work in our lives. We are not the people we once were because of God's saving grace to us in Jesus Christ. There's so much more that could be said about the gospel, but that is what it is in a nutshell.

And that is what Titus is to 'stress' (v. 8). The idea of the word 'stress' is to emphasise emphatically or to speak confidently about or to insist upon. That is what Titus is to do with the gospel. To use an image from boxing, Titus is not to be on the back foot with the gospel, but on the front foot. How is Titus 'to stress these things' or the gospel? He is to do so by teaching and preaching the gospel just as Paul himself does. The gospel is not only a message to be taught, but by its very nature demands to be preached or proclaimed. The gospel must be both confidently and faithfully taught, and enthusiastically and forcefully heralded as the good news that it is – what God has done to save sinners in Jesus Christ. Just as Paul charged

Timothy so Titus too is to 'preach the word … in season and out of season' (2 Tim. 4:2).

And in preaching, Titus will, like Timothy and all preachers, 'correct, rebuke and encourage – with great patience and careful instruction'. That is how Titus is to stress the gospel. Spiritually healthy churches should eagerly desire such preaching and Christians should gladly hear such preaching. What should be desired is not the false teaching that ungodly people want to suit 'their own desires' and scratch their 'itchy ears' (2 Tim. 4:3), but the 'sound doctrine' of the Word of God. And no doubt, like Timothy in Ephesus, Titus is also to train 'reliable people who will also be qualified to teach others' (2 Tim. 2:2).

A little later when we look at verse 14, we will come back to the reason the gospel must be preached in the church, which is 'that those who have trusted in God may devote themselves to doing what is good'. But right now, I want to emphasise how important it is that we keep the gospel at the heart of the church by it being preached.

It is so easy for the gospel not to be at the heart of the church. For sure a church can have a good statement of faith that sums up what the Bible teaches on the gospel, and its leaders and members can all sign it in good faith. But almost imperceptibly the gospel can be moved from the heart of a church to its margins. How does that happen? It happens when it is taken for granted and not treasured as more important than anything else. Other things – often good things in themselves – come to have greater weight in the life of the church. For example, a church can be so involved in doing many good works in the community that they become the big thing in the church rather than the gospel. When that happens spiritual life begins to decline and is replaced by activism that is more about human effort and less the fruit of the gospel.

Another way this can happen is when preaching ceases to be genuinely expository. Rather than let sermons be controlled by the text, the text is used to promote something else on the preacher's mind. That something may not be wrong in itself, but almost imperceptively it is echoing the world and not the Word, at the heart of which is the gospel. However, if the gospel is kept at the heart of the church as it is preached and believed, then among the many things that will happen will be that 'those who have trusted in God' will be encouraged 'to devote themselves to doing what is good'. Preaching that aims to produce that must happen in our main meetings, but also in small groups and in all the ways that the church ministers the gospel to both believers and unbelievers. And not least, we must each individually 'stress these things' or preach the gospel to ourselves so that we are devoted to doing what is good. Such gospel preaching is 'excellent and profitable for everyone'.

2. Avoid false teaching that undermines the gospel

What is not excellent and profitable for everyone are 'foolish controversies and genealogies and arguments and quarrels about the law' (v. 9). What does Paul have in mind here? He is thinking of the arcane debates about the law of Moses.

There was a lot of that among Jews, and some Christians were fascinated by these debates. Many involved speculating about hidden meanings in the Old Testament Scriptures in general and in the genealogies in particular. By the nature of these things a person could easily become obsessively interested in them. They must be 'avoided' because they are 'unprofitable and useless' or empty. Such controversies, arguments and quarrels over genealogies and the law were not harmless. People who, as Paul says in 2:13, pay 'attention to Jewish myths' and 'merely human commands' come to 'reject the truth'. Timothy had to deal with similar people in Ephesus who 'devote themselves to myths and endless genealogies' and 'controversial speculations' and 'meaningless talk' which, far from 'advancing God's work', undermine and contradict it. These people who 'want to be teachers of the law' actually 'do not know what they are talking about or so confidently affirm' (1 Tim. 1:3–6). In fact, Paul says, such people 'abandon the faith and follow deceiving spirits and things taught by demons' (1 Tim. 4:1).

Paul tells Titus to avoid such false teaching. He is to steer clear of it like some dangerous beast. We must do the same. For us, the particular false teaching is most likely to be very different than that which Titus and Timothy faced, but in principle it is the same. For example, the prosperity gospel in its harder versions (you will be healthy and wealthy if you have enough faith) or softer variants (God wants you to feel good about yourself and have a pleasant life) fails to understand what the Bible says about suffering in this world. True prosperity is, in this world, the spiritual prosperity of being a child of God, whatever our physical circumstances. Or there is theological liberalism which takes different forms but basically denies that the Bible is the Word of God to which his people must submit. So for example, we are told that when it comes to human sexuality, the Bible is wrong and that Christians must conform to what the world says and if they don't they should be cancelled. Or there is allowing political ideology, be it from the left or right, or a cause of some kind to supplant the gospel in the life of the church. In these and other ways, churches can depart from the truth of the gospel.

Of course, sometimes theological controversy is necessary for the sake of the gospel. Jesus was a controversialist when he had to be, as were Paul and the other apostles. When a church has to be protected from false teaching, we have to go into battle. But as far as we can, we should avoid getting tangled up in debates with people who claim to be followers of Jesus, but what they teach and love to argue about and debate undermines the gospel. For at best what happens is that we get distracted from gospel ministry. Much of our time and energy is taken up sparring with our opponents in a useless exercise that does no one any good. At worst we can find ourselves ensnared by the false teaching and led astray from the truth of the gospel. Sadly, that continues to happen to good people. We must never forget how dangerous false teaching is to the church. It undermines its foundations and leads to its destruction. So, yes, if necessary, know about false teaching, but be careful not to let it undermine your faith in Jesus as offered in the gospel.

3. Maintain gospel integrity in the church

Sadly, sometimes false teachers gain entry to churches and with their false teaching seek to divide them. Often these people belong to churches. When that happens, the false teachers must not be tolerated, as sadly they all too often are, but rather dealt with firmly and decisively. 'Warn a divisive person once, and then warn them a second time. After that have nothing to do with them' (v. 10).

The 'divisive person' is not merely someone who foments disunity in a church, but someone who divides it with false doctrine. We get our word 'heresy' from the Greek word translated 'divisive'. It means someone who creates factions because of their opinions. Usually, we think of church discipline in relation to people whose behaviour is not in line with the gospel. But church discipline also applies to people whose beliefs are not in line with the gospel. Like anyone who sins, false teachers must be dealt with in the way Jesus says in Matthew 18:15–17,

> If your brother or sister sins, go and point out their fault, just between the two of you. If they listen to you, you have won them over. But if they will not listen, take one or two others along, so that 'every matter may be established by the testimony of two or three witnesses.' If they still refuse to listen, tell it to the church; and if they refuse to listen even to the church, treat them as you would a pagan or a tax collector.

So, in keeping with that process, the false teachers must be warned once, and if they don't repent, warned again and if even then they don't repent, the church is told so that church members can remove them from membership. After that believers should 'have nothing to do with them'. When that happens, we know that the false teachers are 'warped and sinful; they are self-condemned' (v. 11). That is, because of this sin they have brought this judgment on themselves.

That sounds very harsh, but nothing less is required if gospel integrity is to be maintained in a church. Failure to do this has resulted in churches and denominations becoming doctrinally compromised. Sadly, we can see all around us what has happened as a result. It is not loving to tolerate false teaching. One orthodox Anglican bishop speaks of 'the cruelty of heresy' because of the way it corrupts the message churches preach with the result that people are led astray and lost.[1] No, hard as it is, false teachers must be dealt with and that may mean putting them out of the church.

That doesn't mean we should be harsh and censorious. While talking straight we can be gentle and courteous. And we must always hope that, like any sinner, false teachers will repent and be restored to the church. But as long as a man or woman persists in dividing a church with his or her false teaching, we must be resolute in dealing with them. If we don't, the gospel integrity of the church will be compromised and the gospel will be hindered in its advance.

4. Work with others and use circumstances for the gospel

At the end of his letters Paul usually mentions people he greets or whose greetings he sends, as well as the various things he and others are doing. This letter to Titus is typical.

> As soon as I send Artemas or Tychicus to you, do your best to come to me at Nicopolis, because I have decided to winter there. Do everything you can to help Zenas the lawyer and Apollos on their way and see that they have everything they need (Verses 12–13).

Because Paul wants Titus to join him in Nicopolis he is planning to send either Artemas or Tychicus to take his place on Crete. We don't know anything about 'Artemas' but thank God for how much unknown people like him have done to advance the gospel. 'Tychicus' was one of Paul's most reliable colleagues to whom he entrusted key jobs. This is how Paul commends him in Colossians 4:7–8,

> Tychicus will tell you all the news about me. He is a dear brother, a faithful minister and fellow servant in the Lord. I am sending him to you for the express purpose that you may know about our circumstances and that he may encourage your hearts.

Every church and ministry needs good, solid and reliable people like Tychicus. But Titus should also expect 'Zenas the Lawyer and Apollos' to pass through on their way somewhere and he is to make sure they have everything they need. Every team needs a lawyer like Zenas as well as a knowledgeable and persuasive preacher like Apollos. This is doubtless the Apollos who worked closely with Paul and whose preaching was so effective in Ephesus and Achaia, as recorded in Acts 18:24–28.

What all this tells us is that in his ministry Paul was not a lone ranger, but a team player. If we are to see the gospel advance, we also need to work with teams. That is what the local church really is, as is its leadership. Teams of people with different gifts and personalities and backgrounds are needed in every church so that the gospel can advance most effectively. And not only do we need to work in teams in the local church, but local churches need to work together to advance the gospel in towns and cities, regions or nations.

However, not only is teamwork important for the advance of the gospel, but so too is how we use our circumstances. Paul's plan is to spend the winter in 'Nicopolis' (v. 12). This Nicopolis – there were at least three – was most likely the one in Epirus on the west coast of what is today Greece. It was a significant port city and Paul had no doubt decided to winter there because of its strategic importance for the gospel. As we can see from the book of Acts, Paul chose the cities he visited carefully so that from them the gospel could spread more widely through regions and along trade routes.

As we think about the advance of the gospel, we need to have Paul's strategic mindset. As churches we need to think about where gospel ministry should be strategically located to reach as many people in our communities and cities and our nation as possible. And each of us needs to think where we can serve the Lord strategically so that working with others in our churches we will get the gospel to more and more people. Where is your 'Nicopolis' right now at this stage of your life with your particular gifts, opportunities and circumstances?

5. Be devoted to doing good because of the gospel

Twice in this passage Paul tells Titus that the believers on Crete must be devoted to doing good. We've looked at verse 8 already, but now in verse 14 Paul writes, 'Our people must learn to devote themselves to doing what is good, in order to provide for urgent needs and not live unproductive lives'. If we trust in God for salvation, we will do good. Doing good or doing good works is the evidence that we have genuine saving faith. Such doing good is first about living 'self-controlled, upright and godly lives in this present age' as we look forward to the return of Jesus (2:12). Indeed, the reason Jesus gave himself to redeem us from wickedness is that we would be 'a people that are his very own, eager to do what is good' (2:14).

Doing good, then, is about godliness. It is about devotion to God actively expressed in a good life empowered by the gospel. In other words, doing good is about every aspect of our lives. One aspect of such godliness is doing good to people in need. That's the emphasis in chapter 3 as Paul encourages us to be godly citizens in our relationships with non-Christians. The 'urgent needs' that we are to 'provide for' are not our own, but those of people who urgently need our help. Like the good Samaritan in the parable of Jesus we are to have mercy on people in need whom we come across in the course of life. We can do that individually and as families as well as a church. And we 'must learn to devote [ourselves] to doing what is good'. That is, we must be very intentional and learn the habit of doing good so that we live productively as the fruit of godliness is produced in our lives.

Such doing of good is necessary for the advance of the gospel. Essential as gospel proclamation is for that to happen, the gospel must also be seen in the way we live as Christians. If it isn't, our message loses its credibility. A Christianity that is all talk and not walk simply won't gain a hearing despite its truthfulness. That doesn't mean we have to be perfect. There are no perfect Christians. But imperfect as we are, as Christians we are being transformed by the gospel so that we are not the people we once were.

Such gospel transformation is a powerful testimony to the truth of the gospel. And that testimony is magnified when ordinary Christians together do good by helping people in need. We have a rich heritage of believers in past generations of Christians who were devoted to doing what is good in ways that helped not only individuals but transformed communities and the nation. Today we can build on that heritage by doing good as the people Jesus has redeemed for that very purpose.

6. Love the family of believers created by the gospel

As he signs off the letter, Paul conveys the greetings of people with him to Titus and sends greetings through him to 'those who love us in the faith' (v. 15). The Greek word for 'love' here means 'brotherly love'. Paul uses this word because he wants us to understand that we belong to a family of believers and as such are to love one another. Love is what is to characterise our relationships as Christians. Love is what binds us together as the family of God. Therefore, we must care for one another and be concerned for the welfare of our brothers and sisters in the faith wherever they are.

Such love is another key element in the advance of the gospel in the world. A loving community of Christians is one of the most powerful and attractive things about genuine Christianity. The world has nothing like it. Other religions have nothing like it. But in churches where the gospel is powerfully at work changing lives for good, there are people who love one another as brothers and sisters in Christ. And love for other Christians is not restricted to local churches but is expressed for Christians around the world, especially when they are in need of some kind.

7. Keep praying for people to be changed for good by God's grace in the gospel

Paul's final words in this letter are 'Grace be with you all' (verse 15). That's what is known as a benediction, which is a brief prayer that simply asks God to bless people. This benediction may be little, but like an atom it has potentially explosive power. Paul's little but explosive prayer is that people will be blessed by God with his grace. Grace is God's undeserved favour to sinners. Grace is what the gospel is about. As Paul has made clear in this letter, but also as his other letters make clear, and as the whole Bible makes clear, God saves sinners from start to finish by his grace in Jesus Christ. And the gospel advances in the world as that grace is made known through the preaching of the Word that like a hammer breaks open unbelieving hearts.

Therefore, we must pray that God will use the preaching of his Word to advance the gospel in the world so that his grace will be with us and with more and more people, so they become Christians. Our prayer is that as Christians we would know more of the life-changing power of God's saving grace, but also that unbelievers would know that as well. That is how genuine Christianity has advanced through history and that is how genuine Christianity continues to advance today. Let's then commit ourselves to prayer and doing what we can where we are in our generation for the advance of the gospel of God's grace in Jesus Christ.

And that is what it means for God's elect to believe and then learn the truth that leads to godliness (1:1). The apostle Paul devoted himself to seeing that happen and we must as well in our generation. But if we are, we must be clear as to what the gospel is and how it is to be kept at the heart the church. The temptation is to think there are quick fixes and that some new thing (or, indeed, old thing) will do the trick when the gospel isn't advancing as quickly as we might expect. For sure we need to examine ourselves and what we're doing. We need to think about how to contextualise the gospel faithfully in the cultures in which we live and serve. But when all is said and done, we simply need to patiently nurture godliness in line with what the apostle Paul told Titus to do back in first century Crete. Our circumstances are very different, but the gospel and the way it advances are fundamentally the same.

Questions for discussion

1. Spend time reflecting on the seven things you and your church can do to advance the gospel so that godliness is nurtured wherever you are.

2. Spend time in praying for a Titus Revolution wherever you are and in parts of the world where you have a particular interest.

Postscript

If you have got this far with reading this book you will have got the message that at the heart of the Christian life and church is godliness. Sadly, for various reasons that is all too often lost sight of amid all the challenges and pressures we face as Christian in this world. But the cultivation of godliness needs to be restored to the heart of the church as well as to our understanding of what it means to be a Christian.

That is what Titus needed to appreciate as he consolidated the work of the gospel on the island of Crete in the first century and that is what we need to appreciate wherever we are as Christians in the twenty-first century. But if this is to happen, we must make sure that the link between godliness and grace is not broken as it can be all too easily. Decoupled from grace, like a train carriage from the locomotive, godliness becomes at best a poor imitation of the real thing. Orthodox in doctrine and life such Christianity loses its joy and becomes increasingly moralistic. The focus of the Christian life is on outward performance and appearance but with little inward motivation.

At its worst the decoupling of godliness from grace leads to a Christianity that is a deceptive counterfeit; 'a form of godliness but denying its power' (2 Tim. 4:5). Paul uses that expression to describe false religion masquerading as the real thing. That's what godliness without grace can become. Outwardly it can look like genuine Christianity but inwardly it is decaying and even dead.

Sadly, church history bears witness to this happening as does much contemporary experience. So, for example, after English and Welsh Dissenters (that is, Presbyterians, Congregationalists and Baptists who did not conform to the established Church of England) gained toleration in 1689, the once doctrinally orthodox and spiritually vital Presbyterians along with some Baptists drifted into Unitarianism in which they denied the doctrine of the Trinity and the deity of Christ. That same thing happened a little later to many Congregationalists in New England. Later still in the nineteenth century many once totally evangelical denominations were seriously corrupted by liberal theology and we live with the devastating consequences today as those denominations decline. In many of these churches the Bible would be read, the creeds recited and well-loved hymns sung and yet this counterfeit form of godliness no longer had power. Why? Because as well as false teaching, the link between godliness and the power of God's grace in the gospel was lost.

What can be done to prevent that happening? Quite simply we must maintain the link between godliness and the grace of God in the gospel. While that means remaining doctrinally and ethically orthodox it also means making sure that our hearts as

Christians are gripped by God's amazing grace. We must never lose sight of the astounding reality that God saves sinners like us. However, that salvation is not only about being born again by the Spirit and trusting in Christ so that we are forgiven on the basis of his finished work when we were converted, but also about what happens every day in our lives until we reach glory. Every day we must appropriate the grace of God in the gospel. In this way the power of the gospel will change us. In this life that change won't be perfect because of the continuing presence of sin in our hearts, but it will be real as the Holy Spirit empowers us to become increasingly godly. That is the power of godliness.

Let me say a word to fellow pastors and preachers or indeed anyone who has responsibility for teaching others. In our preaching and teaching we must make sure that godliness and grace are coupled for the reasons I have just mentioned. Whatever we believe in theory about grace it is all too easy to default to a form of moralism. We may expound a passage of Scripture and even extol God's saving grace but fail to show how it is an ongoing reality in the life of the Christian. The late Jack Miller used to say that pastors need to preach the gospel to themselves every day since when they lay down to sleep the gospel falls out of their heads.[1]

For most of us moralism is our default setting. So, preach the gospel of grace to yourself every day and then as the Lord gives you opportunity preach and teach it in public and private in all its glorious fullness to others. Like John Newton remind yourself that you are a great sinner, but that Jesus is an infinitely greater Saviour.

The takeaway message of this book is this: **put godliness at the heart of your church and your Christian life so that empowered by the Holy Spirit through the gospel of his grace in Jesus Christ you express your devotion to God by doing good for his glory.**

Further reading

The subjects covered in this book are so varied and many that a comprehensive list of books for further reading would be larger than the book itself. I will restrict myself to books on godliness and the Christian life, the letter to Titus and books related to some of the people and events mentioned that will be helpful to general readers.

Godliness and the Christian Life

There are many great books on godliness and the Christian life. Here is a selection of some of the best and most accessible. In addition to them the publisher of this book, Grace Publications, has a great series called 'Grace Essentials' which includes a number of abridged classic works in plain English. Reformation Heritage Books also publish a series of doctrinal and practical booklets entitled 'Cultivating Biblical Godliness'.

Augustine, *Confessions*, trans. R.S. Pine-Cotton (Penguin Books 1961). One of the classic books of Christian spirituality in which Augustine tells how God's grace triumphed in his life.

Jerry Bridges, *The Practice of Godliness* (Nav Press 1983). Good, wise counsel on the godly life based on key texts of Scripture.

John Calvin, *Truth for All Time*, trans. Stuart Olyott (Banner of Truth 1999). Calvin wrote this introduction to the Christian life for ordinary people with the title A *Brief Outline of the Christian Faith*. Move on to his *Institutes of the Christian Religion*, particularly Book III, which is a classic in itself on the Christian life.

Tim Chester, *The Ordinary Hero: Living the Cross and Resurrection* (IVP 2009). A fine book on what grace means in everyday life.

Tim Chester, *You Can Change: God's Transforming Power for Sinful Behaviour and Emotions* (IVP 2008). Very helpful book about the gospel change at the heart of godliness.

Kevin DeYoung, *The Hole in Our Holiness* (Crossway 2014). One of the best modern guides to gospel-centred godly living.

Sinclair Ferguson, *The Christian Life* (Banner of Truth 1981). A wonderful guide to the doctrinal basis of godly Christian living.

Sinclair Ferguson, *Devoted to God* (Banner of Truth 2016). Very helpful exposition of the Bible's teaching on sanctification.

Sinclair Ferguson, *The Trinitarian Devotion of John Owen* (Reformation Trust 2014). A short introduction to John Owen's teaching on the Christian life by another great theologian of the Christian life.

Michael A. G. Haykin, *Ardent Love for Jesus – Learning from the 18th Century Baptist Revival* (Bryntirion Press 2013). Studies in godliness among one denominational tradition that is applicable to everyone.

Timothy Keller, *Prayer – Experiencing Awe and Intimacy with God* (Hodder & Stoughton 2014). Great teaching about prayer, which is at the heart of godliness.

D. Martyn Lloyd-Jones, *Studies in the Sermon on the Mount* (IVP 1977). A classic study on what it means to be a Christian by one of the greatest preachers of the twentieth century.

John Newton, *Select Letters of John Newton* (Banner of Truth 2011). No one did wise, down to earth, gospel-rooted counsel better than the author of 'Amazing Grace'. There are a lot more from where these came from.

Dane C. Ortlund, *Edwards on the Christian Life: Alive to the Beauty of God* (Crossway 2014). Any of the books in this series about the teaching on the Christian life of key theologians of the past is worth reading.

Dane C. Ortlund, *Gentle and Lowly – The Heart of Christ for Sinners and Sufferers* (Crossway 2020). The heart of devotional Puritanism adapted and applied to the present day.

John Owen, *The Holy Spirit*, abridged and edited by RJK Law (Banner of Truth 1998). As well as this classic in modernised English also read in the same series *The Glory of Christ*, *The Mortification of Sin*, *Indwelling Sin*, *Communion with God* and *Spiritual Mindedness*.

J.I. Packer, A *Quest for Godliness: The Puritan Vision of the Christian Life* Crossway Books,1990). In the United Kingdom the book bore the title *Among God's Giants*. In one way or another much of Packer's writings dealt with godliness.

Richard Rushing, ed., *Voices from the Past – Puritan Devotional Readings*, two vol. (Banner of Truth 2009). Superb introduction day-by-day through the year to the riches of Puritan writings on godliness. Use as part of your daily devotions.

J.C. Ryle, *Holiness* (Banner of Truth 2015). A classic on sanctification by a nineteenth century giant that speaks as powerfully today as when it was written. Read also his *Practical Religion*.

William Still, *The World of Grace* (Christian Focus 1998). Not as well-known as he should be, William Still gets to the heart of godliness in these sermons. Read anything by him.

Willem Teellinck, *The Path of True Godliness*, trans. Annemie Godbehere, ed. Joel R. Beeke (Reformation Heritage Books 2003). Practical and heart-warming teaching on godliness from a Dutch Puritan.

Thomas Watson, *The Godly Man's Picture* (Banner of Truth 1992). Straight-forward teaching on godliness by one of the most accessible Puritans.

Rankin Wilbourne, *Union with Christ* (David C. Cook 2016). A fantastic book on a key aspect of godliness that every Christian needs to understand more fully.

The Letter of Titus

John Calvin, *Sermons on Titus*, trans. Robert White (Banner of Truth 2015).

Tim Chester, *Titus for You* (Good Book Company 2014).

Thomas C. Oden, *First and Second Timothy and Titus* in the Interpretation Commentary Series (John Knox Press 1989).

John R.W. Stott, *The Message of 1 Timothy and Titus* in 'The Bible Speaks Today' series (IVP 1996).

Robert Yarborough, *The Letters of Timothy and Titus* in The Pillar Commentary Series (IVP 2018).

Some historical figures, places and events mentioned in the book

Augustine

Gerald Bray, *Augustine on the Christian Life: Transformed by the Power of God* (Crossway 2015).

Chambon-sur-Lignon

Caroline Moorehead, *Village of Secrets: Defying the Nazis in Vichy France* (Vintage 2015).

Corrie ten Boom

Corrie ten Boom, *The Hiding Place* (Hodder & Stoughton 2014).

William & Catherine Booth

Jim Winter, *Travel with William Booth* (Day One 2003).

Archibald Brown

Iain H. Murray, *Archibald G. Brown: Spurgeon's Successor* (Banner of Truth 2011).

John Bunyan

John Bunyan, *Grace Abounding to the Chief of Sinners* (Banner of Truth 2018).

Faith Cook, *A Pilgrim Path: John Bunyan's Journey* (Evangelical Press 2017).

Great Ejection of 1662

Gary Brady, *1662: The Great Ejection: Today's Evangelicalism Rooted in Puritan Persecution* (Evangelical Press 2012).

Sermons of the Great Ejection (Banner of Truth 1962).

Samuel Morley (and many other nineteenth century evangelical social entrepreneurs)

Kathleen Heasman, *Evangelicals in Action* (Geoffrey Bless 1962).

George Muller

Roger Steer, *George Muller: Delighted in God* (Christian Focus 2015).

Neil Summerton, *'I Thanked the Lord, and Asked For More': George Muller's Life and Work* (Brethren Archivists & Historians Network 2022).

John Newton

Jonathan Aitken, *John Newton: From Disgrace to Amazing Grace* (Continuum 2007).

Tony Reinke, *Newton on the Christian Life: To Live Is Christ* (Crossway 2015).

Oloudah Equiano

Oloudah Equiano, *The Interesting Narrative and Other Writings* (Penguin 2003).

Andrew Reed

Ian J. Shaw, *The Greatest is Charity* (Evangelical Press 2005).

Ellen Ranyard

Donald M. Lewis, *Lighten Their Darkness: The Evangelical Mission to Working Class London, 1828-1860* (Paternoster Press 1986).

Lord Shaftesbury (Anthony Ashley Cooper)

Richard Turnbull, *Shaftesbury: The Great Reformer* (Lion 2010).

Georgi Vins

Georgi Vins, *Three Generations of Suffering: A Chronicle of One Family's Persecution in an Atheistic Society* (Lighthouse Trails 2022).

Wang Ming Dao

Leslie Lyall, *Three of China's Mighty Men: Leaders of Chinese Church under persecution* (Christian Focus 2006).

Wang Ming Dao, *A Stone Made Smooth* (Mayflower Christian Books 1981).

William Wilberforce

Kevin Belmonte, *William Wilberforce: A Hero for Humanity* (Zondervan 2007).

John Pollock, *Wilberforce* (Chariot Victor 1986).

William Wilberforce, *William Wilberforce: His Unpublished Spiritual Journals*, ed. Michael D. Mullen (Christian Heritage 2021).

Endnotes

Introduction

1 John Calvin, *Institutes of the Christian Religion*, two volumes, ed. John T. McNeill (Philadelphia: The Westminster Press 1960), vol. I, p. 9.

2 Ibid., I. ii. 1, vol. I, p. 41.

3 Ibid., III.xix,2, vol. I, p. 835.

4 Joel R. Beeke & Mark Jones, A *Puritan Theology: Doctrine for Life* (Grand Rapids, Michigan: Reformation Heritage Books 2012), p. 848.

5 As quoted in ibid., p. 849. Matthew Poole, *Commentary on the Holy Bible* (Banner of Truth Trust: London 1963), vol. 3, p. 800.

6 J. I. Packer, A *Quest for Godliness: The Puritan Vision of the Christian Life* (Wheaton, Ill.: Crossway Books,1990), p. 310. The British version of this book was published with the title *Among God's Giants*. This is a good introduction to a Reformed and Puritan approach to godliness as is *The Devoted Life* edited by Kelly Kapic and Randall Gleason (IVP USA) which contains chapters dedicated to specific works of Puritan spirituality. Better still is to read some Puritan books. Both Banner of Truth and Reformation Heritage Books publish paperback editions of some of the classics, some of which are in modernised English. Grace Publications has a series of abridged and modernised classics. Other Protestant traditions also have a heritage of teaching on godliness. Even if at points we disagree, sometimes seriously, about how godliness is best nurtured, nevertheless we can learn much from Lutheranism, Wesleyanism and classic Pentecostalism. For example, while John Wesley was mistaken on his perfectionism, we cannot but admire his godly example, zeal for holiness and passionate evangelism.

7 Larry W. Hurtado, *Destroyer of the Gods – Early Christian Distinctiveness in the Roman World* (Waco, Texas: Baylor University Press, 2016), pp. 3–4.

8 Tertullian, *Apology* as quoted in *A New Eusebius*, ed. J. Stevenson (London: SPCK, 1960), p. 173.

9 Hurtado, passim.

10 Alan Kreider, *The Patient Ferment of the Early Church – The Improbable Rise of Christianity in the Early Church* (Grand Rapids, Michigan: Baker Academic 2016). Kreider shows how the spiritual vitality of churches attracted non-Christians who were willing to undergo a long process of catechizing in order to be baptised and join them. It was this patient catechizing and simply being living churches that won the empire for Christianity. For an example of how this happened in the case of Augustine of Hippo see Kenneth Brownell 'Learning Christ: some reflections on the recovery of evangelistic catechesis,' *Foundations* 47 (Autumn 2001): 10–19.

Chapter 1

1 Tom Holland, *Dominion – The Making of the Western Mind* (London: Abacas, 2019), pp. 524–5.

Chapter 3

1 CH Spurgeon, 'The Down Grade'. *The Sword and the Trowel* (April 1887), p. 170.

2 Among evangelicals there is a difference of opinion on the status of the elder denominated 'pastor' or minister. Some understand 1 Timothy 5:17 to mean that he is the teaching elder as distinct from the other ruling elders, as opposed to those who see him as simply one of the elders who may be the 'first among equals'.

Chapter 4

1 William Ames, *The Marrow of Theology*, ed. John D. Eusden (Grand Rapids: Baker Books 1997), p. 77.

2 Thomas CV. Oden, *First and Second Timothy and Titus* in the Interpretation Commentary Series (Louisville: John Knox Press, 1989), pp. 114–115.

Chapter 5

1 Josiah Bull, *The Life of John Newton* (Edinburgh: Banner of Truth, 2007), p. 289.
2 Augustine, *Confessions*, Book X Ch. 29 (London, Penguin, 1961) trans. R S Pine-Coffin, p233.

Chapter 6

1 A present-day Wang Ming Dao is Pastor Wang Yi of the Early Rain Reformed Church in Chengdu, China. Because of his faithful ministry and resistance to the demands of the Chinese government he is now in prison. In 2011 the church published, in the spirit of Martin Luther, 95 Theses about the relationship of Christian citizens and churches to government. That along with a statement by Wang Yi in 2018 entitled 'My Declaration of Faithful Disobedience' can be accessed on the Gospel Coalition website at: www.thegospelcoalition.org/article/persecuted-chinese-pastor-issues-declaration-faithful-disobedience/
2 George W. Knight, *The Pastoral Epistles* in the New International Greek Testament Commentary Series (Grand Rapids: William B. Eerdmans, 1992), p. 333.
3 Matthew Parris, *The Times*, 27 December 2008. Academic research confirms the point Parris makes. See Lamin Sanneh, *Disciples of all Nations* (Oxford and New York: Oxford University Press 2008) and Robert D. Woodberry, 'The Missionary Roots of Liberal Democracy', *American Political Science Review*, Vol. 106, No. 2, May 2012.

Chapter 7

1 William Wilberforce is one of the best known Christians to make a deep impact for good on his society. There have been many others. Going no further than nineteenth century Great Britain we can think of Thomas Chalmers, Thomas Guthrie, Elizabeth Fry, Lord Shaftesbury, Samuel Morley and George Muller to mention a few. Indeed activism in doing good was a mark of evangelicalism and was expressed in the many organisations that shaped much of the life of Anglican parishes and Nonconformist chapels.

2   The full title is A *Practical View of the Prevailing Religious System of Professed Christians in the Higher and Middle Classes of this Country, Contrasted with Real Christianity.*

3   John Stott, *The Message of 1 Timothy and Titus: The Life of The Local Church* (Leicester: IVP 1996), p. 202.

4   David B. Calhoun, 'What Bringest Thou' – Tiyo Soga, *Banner of Truth*, March 2021, Issue 690.

Chapter 8

1   C. FitzSimons Allison, *The Cruelty of Heresy* (Harrisburg, Penn.: Morehouse Publishing, 1994). Allison was one of the last orthodox bishops in the Episcopal Church of the United States. Most of the churches in his old diocese (South Carolina) have joined the Anglican Church of North America.

Postscript

1   C. John 'Jack' Miller (1928-1996) was a Presbyterian minister and professor at Westminster Theological Seminary in Philadelphia. After a crisis in his own life and ministry he came to a deeper appreciation of the grace of God in the gospel. He planted New Life Presbyterian Church in Jenkintown, Pennsylvania and founded World Harvest Mission, now known as Serge. Timothy Keller was an elder in Jack's church. In the late 80s and early 90s Jack was the main speaker at a series of conferences at East London Tabernacle that had a significant impact on me and others in coming to more deeply appreciate the grace of God in the gospel.

Also by Grace Publications

Our 'Christian Life' range includes

Students & Church:
Making the most of your time as a student
by Lois Newcombe

When sorrows like sea billows roll
by Brad Franklin

Our 'Grace Essentials' range includes:

Absolutely Basic: The everlasting Righteousness & Regeneration by Horatius Bonar & J. C. Ryle

Biblical Christianity: The institutes of the Christian Religion by John Calvin

Walking with God: Practical Religion by J. C. Ryle

See our website for further details and more books

www.gracepublications.co.uk